Series on the Iraq War and its Consequences – Vol. 3

# BEYOND IRAQ
## The Future of World Order

# Series on the Iraq War and its Consequences
(ISSN: 1793-1711)

*Published*

Vol. 1
*The Iraq War and its Consequences: Thoughts of Nobel Peace Laureates and Eminent Scholars*
edited by Irwin Abrams & Wang Gungwu

*An extraordinary collection of essays on the recently concluded Iraq War by Nobel Peace laureates and leading scholars. The Iraq War and its Consequences is the first and only book that brings together more than 30 Nobel Peace laureates and eminent scholars to offer opinions, analyses and insights on the war that has drawn both widespread opposition and strong support.*

Vol. 2
*Iraq Beyond the Headlines: History, Archaeology, and War*
by Benjamin R Foster, Karen Polinger Foster & Patty Gerstenblith

Vol. 3
*Beyond Iraq: The Future of World Order*
edited by Amitav Acharya & Hiro Katsumata

Series on the Iraq War and its Consequences — Vol. 3

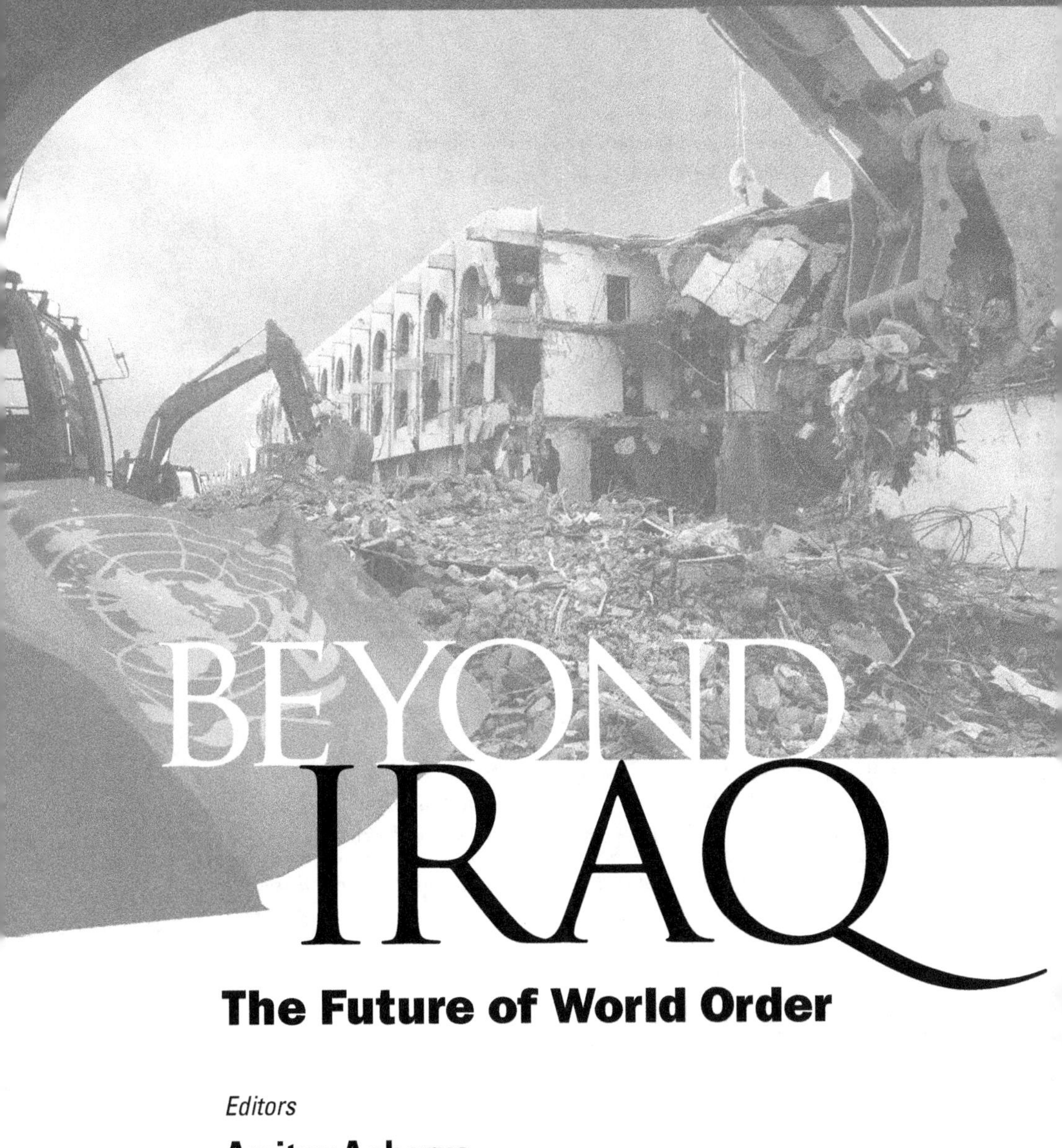

# BEYOND IRAQ

## The Future of World Order

*Editors*

**Amitav Acharya**
*American University, USA*

**Hiro Katsumata**
*Waseda University Institute of Asia-Pacific Studies, Japan*

World Scientific

NEW JERSEY · LONDON · SINGAPORE · BEIJING · SHANGHAI · HONG KONG · TAIPEI · CHENNAI

*Published by*

World Scientific Publishing Co. Pte. Ltd.
5 Toh Tuck Link, Singapore 596224
*USA office:* 27 Warren Street, Suite 401-402, Hackensack, NJ 07601
*UK office:* 57 Shelton Street, Covent Garden, London WC2H 9HE

**British Library Cataloguing-in-Publication Data**
A catalogue record for this book is available from the British Library.

Series on the Iraq War and Its Consequences — Vol. 3
**BEYOND IRAQ**
**The Future of World Order**

Copyright © 2011 by World Scientific Publishing Co. Pte. Ltd.

*All rights reserved. This book, or parts thereof, may not be reproduced in any form or by any means, electronic or mechanical, including photocopying, recording or any information storage and retrieval system now known or to be invented, without written permission from the Publisher.*

For photocopying of material in this volume, please pay a copying fee through the Copyright Clearance Center, Inc., 222 Rosewood Drive, Danvers, MA 01923, USA. In this case permission to photocopy is not required from the publisher.

ISBN-13 978-981-4324-80-9
ISBN-10 981-4324-80-9
ISBN-13 978-981-4324-87-8 (pbk)
ISBN-10 981-4324-87-6 (pbk)

Typeset by Stallion Press
Email: enquiries@stallionpress.com

Printed in Singapore.

# Preface

For the international community, the Iraq War has been one of the most controversial events in the post-Cold War era. Conducted without the approval of the Security Council of the United Nations (UN), on the basis of the erroneous accusation that Saddam Hussein was developing and hiding weapons of mass destruction, this war has divided world opinion. Before and after the launching of a military attack on Iraq by the US and the UK in March–April 2003, anti-war demonstrations were held in various European cities. A majority of UN members expressed their dissatisfaction with the way in which the situation was handled. More significantly, the war even created a rift within the Western alliance, epitomized by the opposition to the attack in 2003 on the part of France and Germany.

Given its controversial nature, this volume aims to explore the implications of the Iraq War for the world order — for an order in Iraq and beyond, in the present era and beyond. It is a collection of essays on topics relevant to the war and international order. Attempts to explore the implications of the Iraq War are by no means novel. A number of authors have offered their interpretations of the cause of the war and its possible consequences. However, unlike many available works on the subject, the present volume seeks to take a broad view and to explore long-term implications of the war, rather than adhering to a narrow view and concentrating on any short-term impact. In this respect, its focus is not only on domestic governance in Iraq, but also on regional governance in the Middle East and global governance. It considers the historical background of the present situation, so as to capture the long-term future trend. Furthermore, it explores not only immediate military strategies but also ideological implications which can have long-term consequences.

All the chapters of this volume are written by leading scholars in their respective fields, who have done a substantial amount of research on relevant issues. While all these chapters offer a professional analysis, they are written for a general audience, avoiding technical terms and scholarly jargon. We hope the readers will find that these chapters offer an objective and rigorous analysis of subjects that have aroused much controversy, such as the role of the US, Islam and religious extremism, without resorting to ideological bias or stereotyping.

This is the third volume in the series of books on the Iraq War and its consequences. The first volume was published in December 2003: *Iraq War and Its Consequences: The Thoughts of Nobel Peace Laureates and Eminent Scholars*, edited by Irwin Abrams and Wang Gungwu. The second was published in August 2005: *Iraq Beyond the Headlines: History, Archaeology, and War*, edited by Benjamin Foster, Karen Polinger Foster, and Patty Gerstenblith. This third volume is presented in the belief that, six years after the publication of the second volume, the time is ripe to explore the long-term implications of the Iraq War for the reconstruction of the world order. It is published under the auspices of the Transnational Governance Initiative of the School of International Service, American University, Washington, D.C. We are grateful to a number of individuals, including our former colleagues at the Department of Politics in the University of Bristol, in the UK.

*Amitav Acharya*
*Hiro Katsumata*

# Contents

| | | |
|---|---|---|
| Preface | | v |
| List of Contributors | | ix |
| Introduction<br>*Hiro Katsumata* | | 1 |
| Chapter 1. | The Future of Iraq<br>*Eric Herring* | 15 |
| Chapter 2. | Regional Order in the Middle East<br>*Louise Fawcett* | 35 |
| Chapter 3. | Just Another Liberal War? Western Interventionism and the Iraq War<br>*Nicholas Kitchen and Michael Cox* | 65 |
| Chapter 4. | The Crisis in Global Governance After the Iraq War<br>*David Armstrong* | 85 |

Chapter 5.  Terrorist Threat in Iraq: Origins, Development
and Impact   109
*Rohan Gunaratna*

Index   149

# List of Contributors

**Amitav Acharya** is Professor of International Relations at American University, USA.

**David Armstrong** is Professor of International Relations at the University of Exeter, UK.

**Michael Cox** is Professor of International Relations and Co-Director of IDEAS at the London School of Economics, UK.

**Louise Fawcett** is University Lecturer in Politics and Fellow of St. Catherine's College, University of Oxford, UK.

**Rohan Gunaratna** is Head of the International Centre for Political Violence and Terrorism Research, Nanyang Technological University, Singapore.

**Eric Herring** is Reader in International Politics at the University of Bristol, UK.

**Hiro Katsumata** is Assistant Professor at the Waseda University Institute of Asia-Pacific Studies, Japan.

**Nicholas Kitchen** is Philippe Roman Fellow at LSE IDEAS, the centre for international affairs, diplomacy and strategy at the London School of Economics, UK.

# Introduction

## Hiro Katsumata

Few events can have a greater impact on international order than wars. Military conflicts symbolize the struggle for power, which is a crucial component of international order. They also signify contestations over norms and ideologies, both of which constitute the basis of politics among nations. This being so, the focus of this volume is on the latest major war in the 21st century, the War in Iraq — the attack by the US and the UK on the country in March–April 2003 and their occupation thereafter. The overall aim of the volume is to explore the future implications of this war for the world order. In what sense can this war be interpreted, and what kinds of problems has it brought about? What are the implications of these problems, and what long-term consequences are in order? What is needed to remedy these problems, so as to reconstruct an order in Iraq and beyond? The present volume is a collection of essays exploring these issues.

The Iraq War has been controversial in many ways. To begin with, the victory has been controversial. It has been widely argued that the US and the UK might have won the war, but not the peace. Certainly their military operation in March–April 2003 was swift and decisive. The gap in military capabilities between the coalition of the two advanced military powers and Iraq was clear, as the latter had been suffering from international economic sanctions for more than a decade. On 20 March, Washington and London launched a military attack on Baghdad, and on 9 April they successfully brought down the dictatorship of Saddam Hussein, ending his rule of 24 years. On

1 May, President George W. Bush made his famous "mission accomplished" speech, in which he effectively declared victory. However, this initial military victory turned out to be the beginning of disaster. The fighting continued, and the reconstruction of the Iraq state stagnated. In addition to military personnel, a growing number of civilians became victims of the war. The new government of Iraq was established in May 2006, but its authority was challenged by various militant groups. Even today, it is hard to argue that domestic order and peace have been firmly restored. Therefore, occupation after the attack in 2003 can hardly be seen as victorious.

Next, the legitimacy of the war has been controversial. This has been a war launched against international public opinion, without the approval of the Security Council of the United Nations (UN). When the US and the UK were preparing for a military attack on Iraq in 2003, international public opinion was overwhelmingly against their position, on the grounds that diplomatic measures to alleviate the tension had not been exhausted. Even in Western Europe, opinion polls showed that a majority of people did not support a military attack and, in various European cities, anti-war demonstrations were held. Within the UN, a majority of members stated that they were against an attack and, more importantly, the Security Council was divided. Amongst the five permanent members of the council, France, Russia and China opposed the position taken by the US and the UK. France, in particular, made it clear that it would veto any resolution to approve a military action, in defiance of Washington and London's attempt to pass such a resolution. In the end, the US and the UK launched an attack without any resolution, and came under severe criticism. Their attack deepened the rift not only within the UN General Assembly and the UN Security Council, but also within the Western alliance of the North Atlantic Treaty Organization (NATO). Within the framework of this alliance, France, Germany and Belgium were among the strongest opponents, while Spain sided with the US and the UK and supported their policy.

The Iraq War may have caused the most severe rift in history within the Western alliance. During the Cold War, the NATO member states were firmly united in their effort to contain the communist bloc. During the first major international crisis in the post-Cold War era, the Gulf War in 1991, these states demonstrated their solidarity in opposing Saddam Hussein's occupation and annexation of Kuwait. Moreover, in the wake of the terrorist attack on 11 September 2001, they acted collectively to give military support to the US-led campaign to oust al-Qaeda and the Taliban from Afghanistan. They did so by invoking, for the first time in the history of the alliance, Article 5 of the NATO Charter — the provision for collective defence, which states that an attack on any member state shall be regarded as an attack on all. Bearing in mind these positive developments, the negative impact of the Iraq War on the Western alliance can be considered unprecedented in scale.

Finally, the purpose of the war has been controversial. Speculation about the purpose of the war has been varied, while the real motive behind the attack remains unclear. The official justification for the military action in 2003 was that the threat of weapons of mass destruction (WMDs) was real. The US and the UK had accused Saddam Hussein of developing WMDs and hiding such weapons from the international inspection team. However, after destroying his regime, they found no WMDs in Iraq. In this respect, the military action in 2003 represented a war on the basis of an erroneous accusation. In addition, the Iraq War may have been part of the US-led global war on terror. The Bush administration had identified the threat of terrorism as the most serious challenge to the national security of the US, after suffering a series of terrorist attacks on 11 September 2001. Before the attack on Iraq, it was widely argued in the US that the regime of Saddam Hussein had links to international terrorist organizations such as al-Qaeda. Yet, since then, the alleged links between Saddam Hussein and these organizations have also been questioned, adding another element to the controversy over the war.

Whatever the case may be, many observers suspect that there were also other motives, which were equally controversial. Most notably, what can be regarded as a conspiracy theory has been proposed, stating that Washington attacked Baghdad with the aim of enhancing the security of Israel and gaining easy access to the petroleum deposits in

Iraq. Closely related to this conspiracy theory is the view that the attack was orchestrated by neo-conservatives to realize their worldview. The ideology of neo-conservatives states that the US should use its military and economic power to promote democracy, human rights and a market economy across the world. Many of the observers, who believe in the influence of neo-conservatives, suspect that these American ideologists had been motivated not only by their worldview but also by their material interests. These observers point out that the neo-conservatives in the Bush administration — such as Vice President Dick Cheney, Secretary of Defense Donald Rumsfeld and Deputy Secretary of Defense Paul Wolfowitz — had close links with Israel and the oil industry. Thus, they suspect that these individuals were concerned with the security of Israel and their vested industrial interests.

Barack Obama, who took office in January 2009, has now been trying to put an end to the war which has caused all these controversies in terms of its victory, legitimacy and purposes. One month after his inauguration, in February, he announced his plan to "responsibly" end the war, by gradually withdrawing US troops from Iraq. According to his plan, by August 2010 the US combat mission in Iraq will have ended, and Iraq Security Forces will have full responsibility for major combat missions. By the end of 2011, all US troops will be removed from the country. It remains to be seen whether or not he will be able to implement his plan without serious difficulties and end the war in a responsible manner.

In any case, the Iraq War must have significant implications for the future world order, and thus any attempt to explore the issue of international order must focus on this war. This is so for three reasons. The first is that the Iraq War is a war in the Middle East. Regional security in the Middle East, an element of which includes stability in Iraq, is an indispensable component for any world order to be constructed. The Middle East constitutes a strategic spot in world politics for several reasons. To begin with, this region is rich in natural resources such as petroleum, and thus almost all the major powers in the world have a stake in it. In addition, this is the region where Jewish state and Arab nations coexist. The management of relations between Israel and its neighboring countries is likely to remain one of the most challenging issues in global governance in the 21st century. Moreover, this region has problems concerning nuclear weapons. Although Saddam Hussein was not hiding WMDs, Israel is commonly seen as having nuclear capabilities, while Iran has in recent years been accused of developing WMDs.

The second reason is that this war is an instance in which the Western powers have attempted to play a part in global governance. The role of the Western powers is another indispensable element of any world order. In particular, the role of the US must be essential, given the country's unmatched military capabilities and economic strength. Yet it should be noted that the unilateral inclination of a superpower might be dangerous because, if such a country were to go out of control or act irresponsibly for its own egoistic benefits, few countries would be able to stop it. To be sure, multilateralism has its limits too. The more actors involved in decision making, the more complicated the process becomes, resulting in the stagnation of multilateral governance. When certain players have the right to veto, multilateral institutions may become incapable of making any decision at all. These institutions may even fail to act decisively in the face of humanitarian catastrophes.

The final reason why the Iraq War must have significant implications for the world order is that this war has been taking place in an area in which Islamic extremist groups have been operating. The management of the threat of terrorism posed by Muslim religious extremists is also an indispensable component of any international order. Within the 21st century thus far, the world has already suffered from a number of terrorist attacks: New York and Washington D.C. on 11 September 2001, Bali on 12 October 2002 and 1 October 2005, Madrid on 11 March 2004, London on 7 July 2005, Mumbai on 11 July 2006, and many more.

## Overall Findings and the Structure of the Volume

Given these features of the Iraq War, the present volume explores the implications of this war for the world order, by covering five specific themes. Thus, it contains five thematic chapters, focusing on the following themes in turn: the future of Iraq (Chapter 1), regional order in the Middle East (Chapter 2), the ideological basis of US intervention (Chapter 3), global governance (Chapter 4), and the terrorist threat in Iraq (Chapter 5).

To be specific, this volume explores the implications of the Iraq War for the world order, in terms of three key issues: (1) domestic order in Iraq and regional order in the Middle East, (2) the role of the Western powers in global governance, and (3) the terrorist threat posed by Muslim religious extremists. The overall findings of the volume can be summarized into three statements:

- *First, the Iraq War has caused numerous long-term security and economic problems in Iraq and the Middle East.* This statement derives from the arguments in Chapters 1 and 2. A variety of security and economic problems in the domestic arena of Iraq are explored in Chapter 1, and those in the Middle Eastern region are examined in Chapter 2.
- *Second, the war has revealed at least two problems in the role played by the Western powers in global governance — namely, their liberal ideology, which justifies a military intervention to impose a liberal form of government, and the emergence of a crisis in global governance.* This statement derives from the arguments in Chapters 3 and 4. It is argued in Chapter 3 that the Iraq War represents a failure of the liberal project of establishing a liberal market democracy; moreover, Western liberals are likely to repeat this same error elsewhere in the future, since they have not recognized their own ideological hubris. It is argued in Chapter 4 that the Iraq War underlines the crisis in global governance today, in terms of its legitimacy and of its effectiveness in solving problems. Yet most of the proposals to improve global governance, such as the idea of reforming the UN, have some limitations.
- *Finally, the war has allowed Muslim religious extremists to challenge the US in Iraq, thereby making this country an important center of terrorism in the world.* This statement derives from the argument in Chapter 5. It is argued in this chapter that an extremist group,

commonly known as "al-Qaeda in Iraq," has been operating in the field, and thus the threat of terrorism is likely to persist; Iraq will probably remain an important global center of terrorism in the foreseeable future. This is the case, although the US has managed to reduce the level of violence in recent years.

While the overall findings of the volume can be summarized into these three statements, each of the five thematic chapters can be read individually for a more thorough understanding of its own theme.

In Chapter 1, Eric Herring of the University of Bristol considers the future of Iraq, by exploring pairs of contrasting perspectives on four key themes. The first theme is history, and the contrasting perspectives here concern historical continuity and change. In many respects, the US-led occupation looks like many other episodes in the history of Iraq, with the extensive use of violence and struggles over political authority and resources. Yet it also has some distinctive features, as Herring points out. In particular, nationalism has proven influential, making it difficult for the US to install a client state. The second theme is politics, and the contrasting perspectives here concern ethno-sectarian identity politics and programmatic politics. In the former, the legitimacy of leaders is based on who they are, whereas in the latter, their legitimacy is based on what they do. The Western media commonly take a primordialist view in focusing on ethno-sectarian identity politics. Under such a view, the toppling of Saddam Hussein in 2003 can be interpreted as taking the lid off the pressure cooker containing ethno-sectarian divisions. The central issue is whether or not there can be compromise between supposedly historically antagonistic groups. However, for Herring, this kind of view is misleading. The Iraq public overwhelmingly rejects ethno-sectarian politics and separation. The political trend since late 2007 has returned to programmatic politics. Thus, there have been efforts to build a nationalist coalition favoring a strong central government. Ultimately, the question for the future of Iraq is not how to separate or reconcile ethno-sectarian groups, but how programmatic politics and ethno-sectarian identity politics will shape each other. The third theme is about the contrast between armed conflict and peace. Herring argues that, since the invasion in 2003, the Iraqis have been at dramatically increased risks of death, injury and other serious forms of harm from indiscriminate violence and persecution. To be sure, the level of violence has fallen since the last quarter of 2007. Yet the country is still unstable, and armed conflict may easily intensify again. The final theme is the economy, and the contrasting perspectives here concern poverty and prosperity. When the US occupied Iraq, the Bush administration openly pursued the goal of making Iraq a neo-liberal economic state, but this project immediately ran into deep trouble. There is still much in the way of neo-liberalization in Iraq, according to Herring.

In Chapter 2, Louise Fawcett of St. Catherine's College in the University of Oxford considers regional order in the Middle East, by exploring three issues: (1) the problems which the Iraq War has given rise to, (2) their long-term implications, and (3) potential remedies. First, she argues that the war has aggravated existing problems and produced new ones in this region. It has stalled political liberalization or democratization in many countries, by providing authoritarian regimes with a reason for not undertaking either. These regimes have limited political liberalism in their dealings with the problem of regime instability resulting from the war — a problem associated with the rise of radical oppositions, sectarianism and jihadism at home. The war has also created regional instability, exacerbated existing regional conflicts, and destabilized the regional balance of power. Furthermore, the unpopularity of the war has weakened the image and credibility of the Western powers, such as the US. Second, Fawcett suggests that the long-term implications of these problems are profound. Democratization is unlikely to progress in this region, and the rise of sectarianism/jihadism will continue to be a threat to regime stability in many countries. The regional security problems caused by the war may intensify the crisis of regional leadership. The absence of strong regional leadership in turn makes conflict resolution harder, and thus may even lead to greater intervention by external powers in regional conflicts. Yet, while these long-term implications seem uniformly negative, with regard to the Western powers' status in the region, pro-Western states such as Saudi Arabia are likely to maintain their close ties with the US. Finally, Fawcett explores potential remedies, including political reform, greater regional leadership and stronger regional institutions. Here she points out that the US will remain a major player. This is partly because other external powers — such as Russia, China and the European Union — have limitations in terms of either their capacity or their willingness to influence the Middle Eastern political scene.

In Chapter 3, Nicholas Kitchen and Michael Cox, both from the London School of Economics, shed light on the ideological basis of US intervention in Iraq: an intellectual framework of what can be regarded as the liberal *zeitgeist*. The Iraq War represents the logical fulfilment of a set of liberal ideas, centered on the notion that democratic states should have the right to intervene militarily in order to protect the rights of individuals in other states. However, although it was a war waged against an illiberal state, the Iraq War created a transatlantic split between American liberals and their European counterparts. Kitchen and Cox offer three reasons for this. First, there was a perception that the US was assuming a dangerous amount of responsibility. Second, the Iraq War came to be viewed as a failure, which exposed flaws in the liberal project of establishing a liberal market democracy. Finally, the Iraq War was perceived as Bush's war. Bush was a polarizing figure who rejected multilateral institutions.

Ultimately, for Kitchen and Cox, the Iraq War was a war of liberal hubris, and of overconfidence in the universal desirability of liberal values. It involved a failure to understand that the right motives do not necessarily lead to the best actions. Nevertheless, liberal policymakers have thus far failed to adequately question the ideological origins of the Iraq War, and their essential link to its catastrophic failure. These liberals have not scrutinized the contradiction inherent in their project that, while aiming to enable people to freely choose their own government, it calls for intervention to impose a liberal form of government, thereby violating the liberal principle of free choice in the first place. Neither have they questioned the assumption that the blessing of liberty would magically produce social stability, prosperity and political consensus overnight. Their post-Iraq response has simply been to look for technical deficiencies, almost as if the task at hand is to learn "how to do it better next time." In this respect, the two authors warn that, in failing to recognize the liberal character of the war, liberals are condemned to repeat the same error.

In Chapter 4, David Armstrong of the University of Exeter focuses on the crisis in global governance today, arguing that this is a crisis of both legitimacy and effectiveness. In the case of Iraq, the legitimacy of the attack led by the US was questioned because it was launched without the approval of the UN Security Council. The UN Charter stipulates that force may only be used legitimately in self-defence or with the approval of the Security Council. Furthermore, the Iraq War may have underlined the fact that the complex challenges in today's world can seldom be resolved effectively by the application of force alone. The consequences of the military attack have been anti-Western sentiments, large-scale internal conflicts, and interventions by external forces such as Iran and al-Qaeda.

After elaborating on the crisis in global governance, Armstrong considers three sets of proposals to improve global governance, and points out their limitations. The first set is based on the ideal of cosmopolitanism, premised on the view that a global community of people can emerge. Such an ideal is hard to put into practice because it is in the first place doubtful whether there are indeed universal moral principles, and whether strong countries will surrender their dominant power to a global community. The second set concerns multilateralism and the rule of law. The implementation of these elements in the global sphere is hard, because major powers would accept a more accountable process of international decision making only when they perceive it to be in their interests to do so. The final set of proposals calls for the reform of the UN. Little progress has been made in this area. To illustrate, the five permanent members of the Security Council commonly use their own power of veto to protect their own interests, and they have resisted proposals to weaken their power in the Council.

In Chapter 5, Rohan Gunaratna of the International Centre for Political Violence and Terrorism Research examines the threat of terrorism in Iraq. His particular focus is on the two most significant threat groups in Iraq: "Ansar al Islam" and "al-Qaeda in Iraq." He traces the origin, development, and international linkages of these two groups, and assesses the impact of their activities. The origin of these groups can be traced to the activities of the Kurdish Islamists in the 1980s. The Kurdish Islamists in Iraq gathered to form the Islamic Movement in Kurdistan (IMK) in 1987, and developed linkages with al-Qaeda in the 1990s. One of the splinters of the IMK, Jund al Islam, evolved into Ansar al Islam in 2001. Ansar al Islam was indeed an associate group of al-Qaeda, and its activities were strongly influenced by this most hunted terrorist group. Ansar al Islam was the host to Tawhid Wal Jihad, a group which relocated from Afghanistan after the US attack in 2001 and which renamed itself Tanzim Qaedat fi Bilad al-Rafidayn, commonly known as "al-Qaeda in Iraq," in 2004.

Gunaratna notes that the decline of al-Qaeda in Iraq began in the mid-2000s, when a number of tribes united to confront this group, and also to confront the Islamic State of Iraq (ISI), which was formed by al-Qaeda in Iraq in 2006. The real turning point came when these tribes started to receive financial support and military advice from the US. In 2007, the US and the tribes managed to reduce violence in Iraq by 80%. However, al-Qaeda in Iraq still remains one of the largest militant organizations in the country, according to Gunaratna. Along with Afghanistan, Iraq continues to witness high levels of violence, and the threat of terrorism is likely to remain a feature of Iraq in the foreseeable future. Ultimately, Iraq will remain an important global center of terrorism for some years.

## The Way Forward: Alternative Views for Lively Policy Debates

Bearing in mind the findings above, what is needed for a reconstruction of the world order for the future? What should be promoted in exploring the way forward to reconstructing an order in Iraq and beyond? The problems in Iraq and the world are complex, and there is no magic formula. Yet it can at least be said that it is crucial to develop alternative views which challenge existing beliefs. In exploring the way forward, nothing should be taken for granted, and assumptions about relevant issues should always be questioned. On the basis of alternative views, lively policy debates may develop, through which better policies may be identified.

This volume is an important source of alternative views. Its thematic chapters offer new perspectives, which challenge existing beliefs about certain crucial issues concerning the future world order. To begin with, in exploring the way forward, an accurate understanding of the domestic political challenge in Iraq is fundamental. On this issue, it is commonly assumed that the central challenge for the future of Iraq is the separation or reconciliation of ethno-sectarian groups with competing identities. Yet, in Chapter 1, Herring underlines the relevance of programmatic politics, to which the central question is the policy implemented by political leaders.

Another important question is who should play a role in restoring order in Iraq and in the Middle East. On this matter, one's focus tends to be limited to the Iraqi government and global players such as the US and the UN. Yet, in Chapter 2, Fawcett argues that regional players may also play an important part. Some Middle Eastern countries should take a leadership role, and regional institutions — such as the League of Arab States, the Gulf Cooperation Council and the Organization of the Islamic Conference — should also be more active. This is because these regional players may enjoy greater legitimacy than Western ones do.

To be sure, the role of the Western powers should not be neglected. In considering their role in global governance in the future, a crucial question to address is the motive behind Washington's attack on Iraq, which caused numerous difficulties. There have been lively debates on this issue. Various strategic considerations have been discussed as possible motives, including the threat of WMDs, the links between Saddam Hussein's regime and the global network of al-Qaeda, the security of Israel and the petroleum deposits in Iraq. Yet, in Chapter 3, Kitchen and Cox shed light on an unexplored aspect of the military action: it was also motivated by the ideological belief that democratic states should have the right to intervene militarily in order to protect the rights of individuals in other states.

Another crucial question is how to improve global governance and to overcome its crisis. There seems to be no shortage of proposals in this area. In particular, a number of proposals to reform the UN have been made, on the grounds that this global organization is dominated by great powers, its operation is inefficient, and it is "undemocratic" because non-governmental organizations (NGOs) are insufficiently engaged. However, in Chapter 4, Armstrong shows that most of the proposals for UN reform are unfeasible or inappropriate. For example, with regard to the idea of making the UN more "democratic," most NGOs are self-appointed, and thus suffer from the same kind of "democratic deficit" which they condemn in the UN.

Finally, in addressing the threat of terrorism in the future, it is essential to examine past mistakes made in the area of counter-terrorism intelligence. In particular, the intelligence errors associated with the military attack in 2003 should be scrutinized. In this regard, many across the world have now come to believe that the alleged links between Saddam Hussein's regime and Osama bin Laden's al-Qaeda were a misconception, and that the disorder after the attack enabled the latter to extend his terrorist network to Iraq. Yet, in Chapter 5, Gunaratna demonstrates that the reality was more complicated than is commonly thought. Osama bin Laden did have a presence in Iraq before the attack in 2003. More significantly, he had established links with a group in Northern Iraq called Ansar al Islam, which opposed the regime of Saddam Hussein.

In democratic settings, alternative views which challenge existing beliefs are always accessible to anyone and readily available. To illustrate, Gunaratna wrote in *The International Herald Tribune* one month before the attack on Iraq that, in debriefing al-Qaeda and Taliban detainees and accessing primary sources, he had found no evidence of Iraqi assistance to al-Qaeda (19 February 2003). Alternative views have been made available in this volume too. What are needed now are lively policy debates in the public sphere, involving both policymakers and citizens. The readers of this volume should actively promote and participate in such debates, thereby playing a role in the reconstruction of the world order.

# Chapter 1

# The Future of Iraq

Eric Herring

## Introduction

What is the future for Iraq? What and who will determine that future and Iraq's position in and impact on the global order? Will there even be an Iraq? Predicting a particular outcome with any confidence is beyond our grasp due to the massive uncertainties involved. Getting futurology right is more luck than judgment, with failed predictions quietly forgotten as somehow not counting and with successful predictions trumpeted. Today's reliable assumptions can become tomorrow's fallacies; or they can be tomorrow's reliable assumptions but next year's fallacies. Timescales matter but are even harder to identify than trends, and the further into the future one attempts to peer, the more speculative the analysis. Specificity matters too: the more specific the attempted prediction, the more useful it will be but the more difficult it is to be right. For example, any society includes diverse social forces which cooperate and compete with each other and in so doing generate new social forces that in turn produce patterns of cooperation and competition that previously would have been regarded as unrealistic or impractical. Futurology suffers from the need to predict — never mind expect — the unexpected. Furthermore, key aspects of the unexpected dimensions of Iraq's future may originate outside Iraq, such as the global financial crisis that began in 2007. Iraq is also part of a feedback loop: the "lessons of Iraq" are being debated globally, and whatever lessons are drawn will have political, economic and military implications for Iraq and its future. Iraq and Iraqis are not merely acted upon. They are also taking actions with significance beyond Iraq's borders.

A more useful way to think about Iraq's future than trying to predict a most likely outcome is to take a thematic approach and in particular to explore pairs of contrasting perspectives on those themes. The value of a prediction lies in whether or not it proves to be true or false, whereas the value of thinking thematically is that one is engaging with the issues that have, at least up to that point, played a role in shaping events. The contrast between predictive and thematic approaches should not be overstated. After all, setting out themes implies an expectation and hence prediction that they will continue to play a role in the future. Equally, predictions about Iraq's future rest on assumptions about those themes and those assumptions are often controversial and some are better grounded than others. A similar caveat applies to the pairing of perspectives on each theme. Although they are set out as contrasting or competing perspectives, it would not be difficult to find elements they share.

The thematic perspectives which will be explored in this discussion of Iraq's future are historical continuity and change; the relative importance of ethno-sectarian and programmatic politics; armed conflict and peace; and poverty and prosperity. The conclusion will then consider the relationships between these themes and ways in which they might interact in relation to Iraq's possible futures within the global order. The overall trend in the world is towards increasing globalization, that is, the various parts of the world are becoming more deeply connected and are increasingly shaping each other in all spheres (military, cultural, economic and political). This means that the future of the local is increasingly tied to the global and vice versa. The global order is the entire set of ideas and practices that structures relations at a worldwide level due to the deliberate choices of actors (states, international organizations, businesses, non-state armed groups, individuals, etc.) and due to the shaping of actors in ways that go beyond their deliberate choices. Globalization is highly uneven and can go into reverse (such as when local or regional interactions intensify and global ones decline), overall or in particular respects. As these are ongoing processes rather than a single event, it makes sense to start with a historical perspective.

## History: Continuity and Change

The question of the extent to which the past shapes the future is a perennial one. Mesopotamia, the historic site of what became Iraq, has for thousands of years been the location of the confluence of and conflict between and within civilizations. Its importance to successive global orders has flowed from its strategic location between Europe and Asia, its resources, its religious significance and the advanced nature of its ideas such as the invention of writing. Many empires have fought over its territory. What became modern Iraq emerged gradually from the integration of the provinces around Mosul in the north, Baghdad in the center and Basra in the south under Ottoman rule. Britain occupied this territory during the First World War, which among other things ended the Ottoman Empire based in what became modern Turkey. Britain exercised a League of Nations mandate to run this territory in 1920, the League being the forerunner of the United Nations but without the US as a member. However, the League collapsed at the beginning of World War Two. Britain then created a monarchy through which it sought to retain control indirectly, and Iraq attained formal independent statehood in 1932. British forces invaded Iraq again in 1941 during the Second World War to secure oil supplies, and withdrew again in 1947 while still attempting to retain indirect control. There followed a series of coups — in 1958 by Brigadier General Abdul Karim Qassim; in 1963 by Colonel Abdul Salam Arif who, after his death in 1966, was succeeded by his brother Abdul Rahman; and in 1968 by the Baath Party, which nationalized the Iraqi Petroleum Company in 1972 and hence had huge resources at its disposal.

Within the Baath Party, Saddam Hussein gradually consolidated his power and became president in 1979. He conducted a bloody, expensive and inconclusive war with Iran throughout the 1980s and ordered the invasion of Kuwait in 1990, only to be expelled by force by a US-led UN coalition in 1991. The UN economic sanctions which were maintained between 1990 and the US-led invasion in 2003 had devastating economic and social effects. These negative effects were exacerbated by some of the regime's responses to them. Before the invasion Iraq was characterized by a ruling elite that, due to its oil income, was able to rely on varying mixes of extensive social welfare programs (destroyed by the sanctions and the regime's priorities), bribes, extreme repression and, towards the end, increased tribalism and religiosity to stay in control. The state was to a great extent run by a set of shadow networks of patronage and corruption that was more important than the state's formal institutions.

The expectation of the administration of then US President George Bush, Jr., was that it would be able to take control of a strong, functioning state that it could hand over quickly to pro-US elected Iraqi exiles. This expectation was fundamentally misconceived. The state had been distorted, weakened and bypassed by Saddam Hussein's regime. There was little loyalty to it, and when the regime was toppled most of what remained of the state collapsed. When the US realized its mistake after the invasion in March 2003, it sought to run Iraq itself to transform it top-down into a liberal democracy with an open market economy which would also be a close ally. However, this extraordinarily ambitious vision was not matched with anything like the resources necessary to achieve it, if indeed it was ever achievable. The collapse of most institutions of the state plus the dismantling by the US of much of what remained in order to try to eliminate opposition contributed to the emergence of armed opposition to the US presence and the new state it was trying to create.

In many respects the US-led occupation looks like many other episodes in Iraq's history, with the interaction of internal and external alliances, the extensive use of violence and struggles over political authority and resources. However, nationalism, the delegitimation of formal empire and the new weight being given to the notion of the sovereign national state with at least formal final say over its own territory have proven influential. These ideas, which are part of the global order, are obstacles to the installation by a mix of force and consent in Iraq by the United States of a client state (that is, one that is generally deferential to the preferences of the invader). Another obstacle to the US achieving its goals is that many groups and leaders dispute where overall political authority lies and procedures for resolving such disputes are often not accepted, so there have been numerous armed power struggles. This is an inherently unstable situation. The interaction of ethnic, religious, sectarian, tribal, class, strategic and political factors in the context of fundamental disagreement over political authority and opportunistic action by those motivated by private gain means that there is strong propensity to resort to organized violence in Iraq.

## Politics: Ethno-Sectarianism and Policy Programs

In identity politics, support for and the legitimacy of leaders are based on who they are. Ethno-sectarian identity politics refers to politics focused on the boundaries and markers of groups which combine perceived or actual shared ethnic and sectarian characteristics. Sect is the sub-division of a religion (for example, Sunnism and Shiism within Islam), while ethnicity involves a diverse set of cultural elements that can include sect. In programmatic politics, the support for and the legitimacy of leaders are based on what they propose to do and actually do. Identity politics and programmatic politics overlap, especially when policy programs focus on what leaders have done or will do in relation to identity politics. Furthermore, in a sense, all politics is identity politics: what you do says a lot about, and shapes, who you are. Nevertheless, there are important differences between the two, most noticeably when policy programs emphasize the delivery of material and status benefits to all citizens of a society rather than strengthening the boundaries and markers of particular ethnic and/or sectarian identity groups within them.

Much media and political commentary on Iraq assumes that there are in effect no Iraqis — that Iraq is composed of around 55% Shia, 25% Sunnis, 15% Kurds and various others; that the population identifies mainly with these groups; and that the violence is mainly between the Shia concentrated mainly in the south, Sunnis in the center and Kurds in the north. This perspective is known as primordialism, meaning that the markers and boundaries of identity are seen as more or less fixed, natural, objective and obvious and as the main determinant of politics.

The Sunni–Shia divide in Islam has its origins in the dispute over the succession to the Prophet Muhammad after his death in 632. Muhammad said he was merely God's messenger in passing on the commandments that formed the basis of the Quran to which people should submit (in Arabic *islam*). Muhammad said that Jesus was not the son of God, but was the closest of all men to God, much closer than Muhammad himself, and communicating the same message. The partisans (in Arabic *shia*) of Ali favored as Muhammad's successor Ali ibn Abi Talib, who was son-in-law and cousin of Muhammad and who was killed in 661 by a former supporter. In contrast, the other Muslims supported succession via a line of caliphs (meaning successors), including Ali as the fourth of these, after Abu Bakr, Umar and Uthman. These Muslims became known as Sunnis, in reference to the Arabic for tradition, *sunna*. The fifth caliph, Muawiyah, ensured that his son Yazid would succeed him, and this occurred in 680. A revolt was led by Ali's son (and hence grandson of Muhammad) Husain. He was soon killed by Sunnis, but the Shia have continued to dispute the succession ever since and regard the failure of many Shia to rally to Husain's side, thus ensuring what they see as his martyrdom, as a matter of everlasting, intense regret and sorrow. In the centuries since, the Shia sect has evolved to have a much more hierarchical and formal authority structure than Sunni Islam.

While the word "Iraq" has been in existence in Arabic (*al-Iraq*) for many centuries (possibly having its origins in a Persian word meaning lowlands), Iraq's creation as a modern state was a product of the British occupation and then its League of Nations mandate. Seen by primordialists as being forced together by Britain and then held together by repressive externally-backed rulers, the toppling of Saddam Hussein in 2003 meant, according to this view, that the lid was taken off the pressure cooker containing ethno-sectarian divisions: Sunnis went from being the rulers of Iraq to a subordinate minority ruled by Shia, with Kurds managing to carve out semi-independence.

From the primordialist perspective, the central issue for Iraq's future is whether or not there can be compromise between these supposedly historically antagonistic groups. The most common suggestion is the idea of soft partition involving a relatively weak central government in Baghdad and three powerful regions with an agreed share of oil revenues. Less commonly, the argument is made for the hard partition of Iraq into separate sovereign, independent states — either an independent Kurdistan and a Sunni and Shia Arab Iraq, or three states, Kurdish, Sunni and Shia. Primordialists assume that once boundaries are lined up with ethno-sectarian identity, internal peace will be much more likely although conflict between these new entities could still occur. This view is a staple of Western news media coverage and has been articulated by then US Senator and now US Vice-President Joe Biden and to a lesser extent by US President Barack Obama.

Despite the popularity in the West of this primordialist application of an ethno-sectarian framing to the point that it is mostly seen as common sense, it is misleading. To begin with, even the categories being used are confusing. The labels Sunni and Shia refer to religious sects within Islam, whereas Kurdish is an ethnic category. Most Kurds are Sunnis (some are Shia), and so it makes no sense to refer to Kurds versus Sunnis. The majority ethnic group in Iraq is Arab and its language is Arabic, an identity marker shared by most Sunnis and Shia. The next biggest ethnic group in Iraq is the Kurds, whose first language is generally Kurdish (which has two main dialects, Sorani in central Kurdistan which uses Arabic script and Kurmanji in northern Kurdistan which, like English, uses Latin script) though many can also speak Arabic.

Far from having a historic inability to coexist, Sunni and Shia Arabs have had few episodes of violence between them in the territory of what is now Iraq, and outside powers have generally been involved in those episodes. Saddam Hussein provided material benefits or inflicted repression according to his assessment of who was a threat and what he thought would control them. Many Sunni Arabs suffered while some Shia and Kurds benefited, even if Shia and Kurds suffered disproportionately. In other words, Saddam Hussein did not simply run Iraq for his fellow Sunni Arabs. The predominantly Kurdish northeast of Iraq has been effectively autonomous since the Gulf War of 1991 when Iraqi forces were forcibly expelled from Kuwait by a US-led UN coalition. However, this Kurdish Autonomous Region (KAR) is not inhabited by a unified Kurdish identity group seeking independence. Since 1991, two secular political parties — the Kurdistan Democratic Party (KDP) led by Massoud Barzani and the Patriotic Union of Kurdistan (PUK) led by Iraqi President Jalal Talibani — have controlled separate parts of the KAR. They fought each other intermittently throughout the 1990s and especially in 1994. Even though Saddam Hussein ordered the use of chemical weapons against the Kurds of Halabja in 1988 as part of his brutal Anfal campaign to crush potential Kurdish opposition permanently, the KDP allied with Saddam Hussein's forces in 1996 to help them in their fight against the PUK, while the PUK in turn allied with Iran against them. Cooperation between the KDP and PUK in the running of the KAR has increased since 2005, but the KAR is a long way from having a fully unified regional government. Despite an underlying preference for a unified independent Kurdistan, the dominant view among Kurds is that a move towards formal independence is far too risky due to the potential for military action by Turkey, Iran or even Syria as well as Arab Iraq to try to stop it or to ensure that major oilfields and the cities of Kirkuk and Mosul are not part of it. In much of the center of Iraq, as indicated earlier, the fighting is mainly among Sunni Arab groups with different objectives, strategies and tactics grouped loosely around the Islamic State of Iraq (ISI), Reform and Jihad Front (RJF) and the Awakenings Movement. These groups are discussed further in the next section of this chapter. In Baghdad, parts of central Iraq and all of southern Iraq, the main fighting since late 2007 has been among Shia Arabs, principally Iraqi government forces loyal to the Islamic Supreme Council of Iraq (ISCI, which was known until May 2007 as the Supreme Council for the Islamic Revolution in Iraq or SCIRI) and those claiming loyalty to the Mahdi Army nominally headed by Moqtada al-Sadr and also the Fadila Party, a splinter from the Sadr Movement. The Iraqi public overwhelmingly rejects ethno-sectarian politics. For example, in an opinion poll in August

2007, 98% said they were opposed to ethno-sectarian separation and 89% said the separation that had occurred had been mainly forcible. In the same poll, 62% of Shia and 15% of Kurds as well as 92% of Sunni Arabs said that they were in favor of attacks on US-led Coalition forces. In February 2007, 61% of those polled said they saw themselves as just Muslims rather than Shia or Sunni Muslims.

The prominence of parties and militias that are almost exclusively Sunni or Shia in central and southern Iraq since the invasion is not a historically consistent feature of Iraqi politics (for example, Iraqi tribes, which are effectively extended families and still play an important role in Iraq, often have Sunni and Shia elements) and does not reflect the views of most Iraqis. Nevertheless, the dominant political parties and groupings are within sects rather than being non-sectarian. The main reason for this paradox is that when the Iraqi state effectively ceased to function after the invasion (in part it collapsed, in part the US abolished it and sought to rule directly whilst trying to create a new state), the social movements which had the most economic power and organizational capacity and which were therefore best placed to step in and replace the state and then establish political parties were ethno-sectarian in character. These social movements have been quite localized and have found sectarian identity to be a valuable legitimizing discourse less because of its inherent appeal than because of a perception of the need to engage in self-defence from those carrying out persecution at least ostensibly on the basis of sect.

Desire for revenge and escalating cycles of revenge further fuelled the explosion of sectarian violence in 2006 and 2007, and local sectarian separation (which was itself usually a product of violence or fear) as a consequence helped to reduce the violence from late 2007 onwards. It can be difficult to distinguish between violence motivated by a commitment to ethno-sectarian politics and gangsterism flying a sectarian flag of convenience. Opportunist thugs who murder their neighbors or terrorize them into fleeing and then take control of their property with a sectarian justification are more likely to be allowed to keep their ill-gotten gains. Fear of persecution on either basis has forced many to vote reluctantly for the lesser of two evils. Even then, the mobilization has not been straightforwardly sectarian, which is why, for example, Shia have lent their votes to a range of parties according to their policies on many issues such as whether to work with or fight against the US-led occupation and whether to have a strong or weak central government. Although a natural affinity between Iraqi and Iranian Shia is often asserted in commentaries by some Iraqis as well as by some outsiders, the possible binding effects of shared sect is mostly over-ridden by a mutual suspicion between Iraqi Shia and Iranian Shia produced by nationalism, rivalry, memories of the horrors of the Iran–Iraq War in the 1980s and commitments to Arab identity politics (most Iranians are ethnically Persian, not Arab).

The notion that there is no going back — that people cannot live together — once there has been ethnic or sectarian mobilization and violence is excessively negative. Most Iraqis have shown limited and usually secondary commitment to ethno-sectarianism, and the political trend since late 2007 has been back towards programmatic politics. This can be seen most clearly in efforts to build a nationalist coalition favoring rapid and full US military withdrawal from Iraq and a strong central government with control of oil revenues. Those trying to develop this coalition have included supporters of Moqtada al-Sadr (Shia Arab), Fadila (Shia Arab), the National Dialogue Front (mainly Sunni Arab but also including Christians) and the Iraqi National List (non-sectarian and mostly Arab). In contrast, the KDP and PUK (Kurdish) and ISCI (Shia Arab) have favored a slower US military withdrawal and more power to regional governments, including control over much of the oil revenues. The more nationalist, centralist coalition has not managed to develop much in the way of unity, but the point is that, however messy, Iraqi politics is not reducible to ethno-sectarianism and the programmatic perspective is an indispensable part of the picture. Hence, the question for Iraq's future is not how to separate or reconcile the members of supposedly fixed, distinct and antagonistic ethno-sectarian groups, but how fluid, overlapping and ambivalent ethno-sectarian identities and programmatic politics will shape each other. However difficult it may be to answer this question, at least it is the right one. A central element of that answer will relate to decisions about whether and how to resort to armed conflict or to pursue goals through peaceful means.

## Armed Conflict and Peace

Since the invasion in 2003, Iraqis have been at dramatically increased risks of death, injury and other serious harm from indiscriminate violence and persecution by a wide range of parties using a multitude of means. The small, voluntary civil society group Iraq Body Count (IBC) which gathers data daily on civilian deaths reported in the news media has counted over 91,000 violent civilian deaths since the invasion phase to the end of April 2009. Many other deaths have gone unreported, and estimates of the total number of additional deaths of Iraqis (including disruption of health care) are many times, including ten times or more, higher than the IBC count. What is certain is that Iraqis have also suffered from many human rights abuses and when the people have suffered injury or physical or mental ill-health, they have been at severe risk, increased since the invasion, from the consequences of insufficient medical care. These risks from the actions of US-led Coalition forces, Iraqi government forces, private security forces, insurgents, militias and criminals and from inadequate infrastructure are not evenly distributed geographically. Iraq is divided administratively into 18 provinces (also known as governorates). Attempting to relocate to a relatively safe province of the country without legal authorization for entry and residence has involved problems in relation to securing food and shelter, and creates the risk of arrest, arbitrary detention, torture or death by Coalition, Iraqi government and militia forces, especially when lack of legal status leads to the suspicion that the person might be an insurgent. Despite this, around 2.7 million Iraqis have fled to other parts of Iraq since 2003 and another two million-plus have fled abroad, mainly to Syria and Jordan. Although a small number have returned to their homes since late 2007, some displacement has continued to occur. The sharp fall from late 2007 onwards of the rate of deaths counted by IBC has been broadly maintained, but this still amounted to 370 violent civilian deaths in May 2010.

Serious risks of one form or another exist throughout Iraq for the population. Even in the KAR, the most peaceful part of Iraq, the KDP and PUK run their own security forces which routinely engage in torture and denial of due process. There is great potential for escalation over the future of the city of Kirkuk and the province of the same name. With 750,000 people, it is Iraq's fourth largest city after Baghdad, Basra and Mosul. The largest group in Kirkuk is the Kurds, followed by the Arabs and Turkmen and a relatively small number of Assyrians and other Christians. A provincial referendum mandated by the Iraqi constitution on whether Kirkuk with its great oil wealth should become part of the KAR, as most Kurds want, or remain outside it, as the others want, has been postponed repeatedly. This delay is sensible until there can be confidence that the losers, or indeed the winners, will not turn to violence or until a compromise can be found. Furthermore, the issue of what constitutes the legitimate voting community has been complicated by the fact that under Saddam Hussein, the province and especially the city of Kirkuk had been partially Arabized, with hundreds of thousands of Kurds forced out and replaced by Arabs, mainly Shia, and this Arabization has been only partly reversed since the invasion.

Trying to assess possible futures for Iraq is made more difficult by the fact that Iraq has been the site of multiple evolving armed conflicts since 2003 rather than a single conflict between two distinct sides. The combatants have included Coalition and Iraqi government forces; private commercial security forces; the Kurdish *pershmerga* (as the PUK and KDP fighters are known); ISCI's Badr Organization; the Mahdi Army; the Fadila Party militia; the tribal, insurgent and local militias that make up the Awakening Councils; the groups in the RJF; and the groups under the ISI umbrella. Many of the groups are internally divided or are so loose in their structure that local forces supposedly under central command are actually autonomous.

The difficulty of considering possible futures is further exacerbated by the fact that the line between government forces, insurgents, party militias, tribal militias, neighborhood militias and criminal armed gangs is blurred. Hence, trying to strengthen the state by providing weapons, training, intelligence and other support may actually strengthen militias, insurgents and criminals who will use these resources for their own ends. Cooperation with and integration into the state by these groups may turn out to be tactical and short-term.

The fluid and unpredictable patterns of armed conflict in Iraq can be seen in the changes within the mainly Sunni Arab aspect of the insurgency (an insurgency being an armed attempt to overthrow a state, in this case one being established in cooperation with foreign invaders). There has been a nationalist Sunni Arab insurgent trend aimed at creating a new Iraqi state within its present borders and a more salafist Islamist Sunni Arab trend aimed at creating an Islamic caliphate, that is, a confederation of territories ruled not by a modern state according to a constitution but by clerics ruling on the basis of the Quran and related Islamist thought. For these *salafi* (meaning ancestors, emphasizing their claim of the purity and unity of early Islam before the Shiism), the Shia branch of Islam is a betrayal of the true Islam. They engage in *takfir* (excommunication) of Shia, declaring them to be *kuffar* (unbelievers in or concealers of the truth) who may be expelled or killed. The decision of the salafists to announce the formation of an Islamic State of Iraq (ISI) in 2006 and to attack other Sunni Arab insurgents was a huge miscalculation (so much for the ISI's attempt at futurology) and produced a further split. The Awakenings Movement — referred to as the Sons of Iraq by the US government — of tribal and neighborhood militias emerged to a great extent from within the insurgency. It offered to cease its attacks on US and Iraqi government forces in exchange for their financial and military support while the Awakenings Movement fought the ISI. In contrast, the Reform and Jihad Front (RJF) of Sunni Arab insurgents which emerged in 2007 is officially as opposed to the US and Iraqi government forces as to the ISI, although it has turned out to be willing to engage in some cooperation with the US and its Iraqi allies. These types of twists and turns can be explained in retrospect but cannot be predicted with any confidence. The heavy defeats that the ISI have suffered since 2006 suggest that there will be a reduced emphasis on disputes over religious ideology between and within Islamic sects in the near future in the dynamics of Iraqi politics, but beyond that its significance is unclear and that trend may be reversed.

On the basis of violent civilian deaths confirmed in the news media and collated by IBC (and as pointed out earlier, the real death toll among Iraqis from violence and indirect costs of violence could be multiples of this figure), the violence in Iraq has fallen a great deal since the last quarter of 2007. IBC's figures peaked at around 26,000 civilian deaths in 2006 and at around 23,000 in 2007 to around 8,000 in 2008, and an extrapolation of the count for the first quarter of 2009 to the whole year would produce a figure of around 5,000. In most cases of the deaths in 2008 and 2009 it is not possible to be clear who caused them, although it seems that fewer than 10% were caused by US or other Coalition forces. At least a substantial minority of the killings have been anti-occupation in motivation, that is, aimed at trying to drive out US forces and to inflict harm on those working with the United States. With US forces scheduled to leave Iraq anyway, the attacks seem mainly aimed at hurting Shia and Kurds for their domination of the Iraqi government through Shia and Kurdish parties, with little hope that the government can be brought down or altered much. Although the formal occupation ended in 2004 with legal sovereignty transferred to the Iraqi government, the US has continued to play a major military and to a lesser degree political and economic role in Iraq.

The reduction in violence since the last quarter of 2007 had a limited relationship to the Bush administration's new security strategy known as the "surge" of providing additional troops whilst increasing controls on freedom of movement to make attacks more difficult and pressing for political reconciliation. There has been limited progress on political reconciliation. The surge had its greatest impact on the Mahdi Army, which decided to suspend armed operations officially and agree to a ceasefire with ISCI in late 2007 but was then targeted by a US–Iraqi government (and hence ISCI) offensive in 2008. The two other main factors underlying the reduction in violence is that there has been a massive amount of forced sectarian separation and also that many Sunni Arabs decided to turn their guns away from the US and its Iraqi allies in order to deal with the greater immediate threat from the ISI. This development, which the US has been happy to encourage and about which the Iraqi government is much more suspicious, is fortuitous rather than a deliberate product of US strategy.

The United States, meanwhile, had been hoping for a long-term military presence in Iraq and had insisted that its withdrawal of troops would be dependent on conditions (Iraqi state security forces being strong enough to cope) rather than a fixed timetable. However, in late 2008 the US had to accept a vote by the Iraqi parliament requiring all US combat forces to leave Iraqi cities, villages and localities and withdraw to their bases within Iraq by the end of June 2009, and requiring all US forces of any kind to leave Iraq completely by the end of 2011, with this decision to be put to a national referendum for approval before the end of July 2009. Some, notably the Sadr Movement, are pressing for a more rapid US withdrawal. The US also had to agree that it would not in the meantime use Iraqi territory to attack other states — there had been a concern that the US would attack Iran using bases in Iraq — and that all military operations would have to have Iraqi approval.

Public opinion polls show that most Iraqis have been of the view that the US presence has made security worse rather than better and that security will improve when US combat forces leave. Most would be happy to have the US provide training for Iraqi security forces. However, there is disquiet among some Iraqis over the elite Iraq Special Operations Forces (ISOF) because it has US advisors at every level of command and it is outside the normal Ministries of Defence and Interior command structures, answerable directly to the office of Prime Minister Nour al-Maliki. The concern is that it is being used as al-Maliki's personal paramilitary force or to serve the interests of the United States. In addition, the government now has formal control of the Awakenings Movement forces and arrests Awakenings militia members it claims are disloyal. It remains to be seen whether truly national, non-partisan security forces are emerging in Iraq or whether the US is effectively backing one faction in an ongoing civil war now operating at a lower intensity than in recent years.

The Obama administration is trying to maximize its military influence and presence within the terms of the withdrawal agreement and also by seeking to alter its terms. The Commander of US forces in Iraq, General Ray Odierno, indicated in June 2009 that US forces would still be deployed in 320 outposts throughout the country to give combat support and technical advice, despite the agreement for all US forces to withdraw to their bases by the end of that month. He also indicated that US combat troops might still operate in Iraq, subject to Iraqi government approval. The Obama administration formally ended the US combat role in Iraq in August 2010 but plans to keep up to 50,000 troops in the country until the end of 2011. The Obama administration has sought to discourage the Iraqi government from holding the agreed referendum on the withdrawal agreement because the agreement states that, if the Iraqi public vote to reject it, US forces will have to withdraw within one year of the vote. As it has turned out, the referendum has become a non-issue with the departure of US combat troops and with US forces concentrating on the relatively popular roles of training and support.

Iraq is still unstable and the patterns of armed conflict and peace have been shifting rapidly and in major ways. Although the overall trend has been for violence to build to a peak in 2006–2007 and decline thereafter, it could easily intensify again or shift to places that have been relatively peaceful. There could also be major shifts in the international dimension in that neighboring states (in particular, Turkey and Iran) might decide to intervene in a much more open and large-scale way. Central to such outcomes will be the political context, in particular with regard to arrangements for the balance of power between central and regional governments, including control of oil revenues, and whether armed groups are integrated into the state or remain outside its control. These trends in violence and politics have influenced, and have been influenced by, the patterns of poverty and prosperity in Iraq discussed next.

## The Economy: Poverty and Prosperity

The huge rise in the price of oil that preceded the global financial crisis which began in 2007 and the crash in oil prices that has accompanied it are significant for a state which receives nearly all of its revenues from oil exports. This will have implications for the rampant corruption within the Iraqi political system as well as for its formal spending programs.

The dominant economic ideology of our time, neo-liberalism, which involves deregulation of business, the opening of economies to external competitors and the reorientation of the state and welfare provision to promoting economic competitiveness, has faced a major setback as global recession resulted in many governments taking a much more strongly regulatory role, nationalizing many banks (at least for the time being) and increasing their spending. This means that a new and unexpected question mark hangs over whether Iraq's future, along with that of the rest of the global order, will be a neo-liberal one. Neo-liberalism has gone through a number of phases already, so perhaps it is not dying but retrenching and changing in form. Liberalism is somewhat different, being a commitment to individual rights and responsibilities in the context of equality of opportunity (something that can at most be approximated in reality), the rule of law, freedom of expression and association, a mainly market economy (again, something that is routinely undermined by things like government subsidies to weaker industries) and governments chosen in multi-party, more or less free elections.

Some see neo-liberal economics and liberalism as closely related, but neo-liberalism is often, sometimes deliberately and sometimes inadvertently, associated with illiberal ideas and practices. This is because neo-liberal policies are often unpopular and so are sometimes imposed, including by force. This has certainly been the case for most Iraqis, who have shown a strong preference for their own control over their economic future rather than having it chosen for them by the United States during the occupation and for extensive state welfare and involvement in the economy. It is significant that the oil contracts offered in 2009 by the Iraqi national government to foreign private and state-owned oil companies are contracts to provide services for a fixed fee as opposed to a percentage share of profits. The Kurdish Regional Government, which favors more neo-liberal contracts in which profits are shared between the Iraqi government and oil companies, has asserted that the new contracts are unconstitutional.

When the US occupied Iraq formally, the Bush administration openly pursued the goal of making Iraq one of the most neo-liberalized states in the world through deregulation, privatization, low taxes on companies and opening up the economy to foreign companies. However, this project immediately ran into deep trouble for many reasons. The numerous nationalized industries were mostly on the brink of collapse due to their inefficiency and mismanagement under Saddam Hussein and many years of economic sanctions; looters caused an enormous amount of damage; criminal gangs, smugglers and corrupt state officials stole a substantial portion of Iraqi oil, oil revenues and other state funds; insurgents were determined to wreck any attempt at economic reconstruction as part of their efforts to drive out the occupiers; reconstruction was so inhibited by security concerns that not much was carried out in comparison with the scale of need; the Bush administration was more interested in appointing people who were politically loyal than competent; the Bush administration put US companies in charge with the result that those companies benefited more than Iraqis did; and anything other than the slow, piecemeal privatization of Iraqi oil was regarded by the US as too dangerous politically to attempt.

There is still much in the way of neo-liberalization in Iraq (in particular, deregulation, low taxes and opening up the economy). Iraq's economic policies need to meet with the approval of global bodies such as the International Monetary Fund (IMF) and World Trade Organization (WTO), and these bodies — both international organizations with their own bureaucracies and made up of states — have a broad commitment to neo-liberalism. IMF approval is an important part of a country's ability to create confidence among international investors even if that country is not seeking IMF loans. The IMF is based in Washington, DC. Its 185 member states, nearly all the states of the world (North Korea, Cuba and a few others are not members), make funds available to the IMF and have votes proportional to the size of their economy. In the case of the WTO based in Geneva, 151 countries are members of it and Iraq is in the process of trying to join. The importance of the WTO lies in the fact that it manages the rules of global trade and so if one country thinks that another country's policies (such as putting taxes on imports to make them less competitive than domestic products) are in breach of WTO rules, it can take its case to the WTO. The WTO can rule one way or another and can require states to change their policies. Hence, even if the direct imposition of neo-liberalism via US occupation has had major setbacks, Iraq is being socialized into the operation of what is in many ways a neo-liberal global order.

The question of development is central to Iraq's future in the global order, and its economic dimensions are strongly bound up with its political and military ones. By the 1980s, Iraq had achieved a great deal of industrialization with widespread health care and education as long as you were not a person or part of a group perceived to be a threat to the regime. War, mismanagement and sanctions turned the clock back significantly even before the invasion, but the disruption since the invasion has been so extreme as to make the poverty in Iraq deeper and more widespread than at any other time in the last 40 years. Displacement, unemployment, malnutrition, loss of access to education and every other measure of the effects of poverty have become the lot of a substantial minority of Iraqis, especially in the center and south where armed conflicts have been most intense. The big question for many Iraqis is whether or not there will be any serious attempt to involve them in dramatically raised levels of prosperity in the future. It may be that they will effectively be left behind by development, seen as entitled to, at most, basic needs for physical survival in a relatively short lifespan as those basic needs are often not met and also to be disciplined by force if necessary to maintain inequality and suppress any rebellious tendencies. This analysis sees the world as divided into the global North (those whose relatively high levels of consumption and welfare provision are defended through measures such as limited aid, border controls and military intervention) versus the global South (those with relatively low levels of consumption and welfare who are treated as potential threats). The word "global" matters here because there are those in the geographical South that are integrated into the network of people benefiting from the current global order, just as there are those in the geographical North that are among those losing out from the current global order.

## Conclusion

It should be clear from this analysis that any attempt at predicting a very specific outcome for Iraq's future would be rash and little more than speculation. Instead, what can be identified are general themes which are focal points of conflict and cooperation. The themes explored in this chapter could be tied together into two competing scenarios, with a long-term pattern of ethno-sectarianism, violence and poverty set against an alternative future of programmatic politics, peace and prosperity, with each element of the two scenarios being mutually reinforcing. This is a possibility, but reality is already rather messy in terms of there being elements of both in play. There are elements of historical continuity and change, ethno-sectarianism and programmatic politics, violence and peace, and poverty and prosperity. Furthermore, it is not necessarily the case that violence and poverty are strongly associated with each other. In armed conflict, there can be winners as well as losers in material terms, and peace can be a product not of prosperity but of acquiescence in poverty through lack of ability to effectively take up arms to challenge it.

Iraq's future will reflect the interaction of Iraq's own distinctive dynamics, regional dynamics and the wider global order. The evidence suggests that Iraq's future will involve violence, struggles over the control of oil and numerous actors pursuing their own interests by working outside the state or through it. Nevertheless, conscious human agency plus the fluidity of the situation within Iraq and right up to the global level reinforce the sense of the future being open-ended and uncertain in many respects.

## Chapter 2

# Regional Order in the Middle East

## Louise Fawcett

### Introduction

This chapter presents an overview and critical interpretation of the development of regional order in the Middle East since the Iraq War. It is plain to even the casual observer that the war and its consequences have produced important changes in and beyond the Middle East. The levels of instability and conflict in an already volatile region have increased. Some states and regimes have been weakened, most notably the Iraqi state itself; others, like Iran and Syria, appear strengthened. There are new regional alliances and relationships between states and powerful radical groups. The region is in a state of flux and its future course remains uncertain.

If identifying changes to regional order at different levels is relatively easy, isolating the source and implications of these changes is less so. Three immediate challenges can be identified:

- First, the notion of order is a contested one. Not all states and peoples share the same conception of order, in particular what a desirable order should comprise.
- Second, there have been a great many developments at many different levels in the region since the US and its allies entered Iraq in 2003. A number of the developments that have occurred may be linked directly to that war; many may also be attributed to other events and processes.

- Third, events in the Middle East continue to move and change rapidly, making any discussion of present and future orders highly speculative. Events in Lebanon since 2006, the situation in Gaza following Israel's intervention in late 2008, or the contested Iranian elections of June 2009 show how the region remains in a state of flux.

The aim of this chapter is to determine not only what kind of order has emerged, but also to highlight which factors best explain change. This analysis, in turn, may also help us to point to the future prospects of regional order and their implications.

If the task is challenging, it is nonetheless important to unravel the different strands of change. The prevailing order in the Middle East is a central component of any global ordering system — an observation that could not be made, at least to the same degree, about other regions of the world. It is also, to some extent, a barometer of global order. The region is too important, from the point of view of its resources, strategic position and cultural make-up, to be disregarded. What happens there, and this has been true since the birth of the modern state system, has profound global repercussions.

Three broad questions frame this discussion about regional order in the Middle East since the Iraq War:

(1) What kinds of problems have the Iraq War given rise to as regards order in the Middle East? What are the opportunities and challenges the war has presented at the regional level?
(2) What are the broader implications of these problems for order in the Middle East? Have they produced major changes, leading, for instance, to a repositioning of key actors and a new balance of power in the region?
(3) What are the potential remedies or solutions to these problems and their wider ramifications? Should these remedies be best sought at a local or international level?

Despite the obvious interdependence between all these questions, the chapter considers each in turn and treats them independently

*Regional Order in the Middle East* 37

where possible. In order to assist the analysis and provide a common framework, each question is considered from three different perspectives: the domestic, intra-regional and extra-regional or global.

Before turning to a more detailed consideration of the above questions, it is useful to briefly discuss how regional order might be understood from a Middle Eastern perspective. For arguably, it is precisely disagreement over the desired nature of any regional order, that lies at the heart of any discussion that attempts to identify problems and their solutions.

## Order in the Middle East: Past and Present

Order, as discussed elsewhere in the volume, is a subjective concept with many possible meanings. One dominant notion of order in International Relations has been that of an idealized Westphalian system — of sovereign independent states existing in a loose international society defined by common rules and norms. Arguably this notion has always been and remains under challenge. Nonetheless, it persists as the dominant ideal for Western states in conceiving of order for the Middle East. Whether it exists today, or whether it has ever existed, as the dominant ideal among Arab states and their populations is debatable. Viewing the strength and importance of non-state actors and movements (whether sub- or supra-state), and the relative weakness of states in the region, it might be speculated that the Middle East system has passed from a pre-Westphalian one, as in the Ottoman Empire period, to a post-Westphalian one, characterized by state fragility and the rise of non-state or transnational groups and institutions, without ever passing through a mature Westphalian phase.

The above may indeed be part of the problem as we try to apply familiar ordering concepts to the region. Order, like the sovereign states that comprise it, is an imported concept, as highlighted by Bertrand Badie in his book *The Imported State: The Westernization of Political Order*. Our concept of order is intimately linked to a particular concept of the state. But that concept of the state today is under challenge, whether from globalization, intervention, or pressures from above and below, and nowhere more so than the Middle East, though whether this challenge is a temporary or more permanent one remains to be seen.

Order in the Middle East has been fluid and contested since the development of the modern state system which followed the defeat and dismemberment of the Ottoman Empire after the First World War. At first it was an order in the making, the parameters of which were largely defined by major external powers like Britain or France. It was a contested order in which many states moved towards independence under some form of colonial tutelage; others already enjoyed formal independence — Iran is one example — but were still subject to the conflicting pressures of external powers.

The Second World War facilitated the move towards independence for most states, though close links to the colonial powers persisted until well into the 1950s and even the 1960s for the Arabian Gulf. The Cold War, however, saw the displacement of colonial tutelage and control with that of the newly emerged superpowers. This provided a new and different dimension to the processes of state and nation building, but its legacy is important when considering the responses of Middle Eastern states today to external acts of intervention. There is necessarily a link made in the minds of many in the contemporary region between the position of powers like the US and UK today to their actions, together with those of other European powers in the inter-war and Cold War period.

During the Cold War and even after, the dominant idea of the Middle East was that of a region with problems but one that with the right combination of cajoling and encouragement — of sticks and carrots — could be persuaded to join the Western society of sovereign states. This idea was tested by ideologies like Arab nationalism and the importance of non-state actors like the PLO; by events like the Iranian revolution of 1978–1979 and the rise of Islamic fundamentalism. All these challenged prevailing notions of order, as would the later events of 9/11, not least in the discovery that even close Western allies like Saudi Arabia were somehow implicated in the "war on terror." However, the notion or the aspiration of a Middle East constructed around a Western model persisted, even through the early years of the Iraq invasion. Indeed Iraq was to be the model of a new order, a beacon for Arab states. Reflecting on the progress of regional order after the 2006 Israel–Hezbollah war in Lebanon, then US Secretary of State Condoleeza Rice described the "birth pangs" of a new Middle East, praising Egypt, Saudi Arabia and Jordan for openly denouncing the radical group Hezbollah. But this image, always fragile, has been repeatedly challenged: by a still powerful Hamas and Hezbollah together with other influential groups like al-Qaeda or the Palestinian Islamic Jihad; by the continued fracture of Palestinian movement, and the weakness of Lebanese, Iraqi and Afghan states; by the prevarication of traditional Arab states, their leaders and institutions; by Israeli insecurity; by Iranian and Syrian pretensions to regional status; and by the derailment of the Arab–Israel peace process.

Rather than order, a new regional disorder might be a more appropriate label for the Middle East as the first decade of the 21st century draws to a close. Indeed, a recent book by Tzvetan Todorov finds that the war on terror and the Iraq War have together provided significant components for *The New World Disorder* it describes.

At one level, however, such conceptions of order and disorder are too simple; there was never one single identifiable order before the Iraq War. And since the war started, different and often competing visions of order have jostled for position. Furthermore, and a concern of this chapter, how much can changes brought about by the Iraq War explain the region's current situation? Or is change post-Iraq linked to change post-9/11 or even earlier to broader changes that can be identified since the end of the Cold War?

One point is clear as we move to consider the region since the Iraq War: any single vision of Middle Eastern order, whether past, present or future, cannot be taken for granted, and that even as we discuss the topic our conceptions of order are changing. Today, however, the challenges to or alternatively an appreciation of the failures of the Westphalian model when applied to the Middle East are particularly striking. One might speculate, not just in the Middle East but in other regions of the world where sub- and supra-state forces and groups enjoy increasingly predominant roles, that it is increasingly hard to still conceive of order in such terms.

## The Iraq War and Order: Problems

To state that the Iraq War has introduced important changes and new problems to regional order is to state the obvious. The world's media has been full of stories of the war's failure to achieve its goals and its damaging consequences for the region and wider world. Yet it is important to point out that the Iraq War was designed to remove, rather than exacerbate, problems. It aimed to reform Iraq's political regime, to promote it as democratic, liberal and tolerant: a model to influence the development of other like-minded regimes. As such, it was also designed to play a role in easing regional conflicts and promote peace. In short, regime change in Iraq would pave the way for responsible government and international relations throughout the region. It would also reduce the threat of nuclear proliferation and facilitate the ongoing war on terror by undermining the position of those states which supported terrorist groups. Finally, by achieving these goals and fostering a more stable regional society, it would also promote better understanding and communication between Middle Eastern and Western regimes and assist thereby in the construction of a more stable international order.

What is most striking about a consideration of the development of order in the Middle East since the Iraq War, is that in none of these areas have the desired changes been achieved either in the short or medium term, making more distant the prospects for a longer-term improvement in regional order. The French journalist and writer on the Middle East, Alain Gresh, has argued that not since the 1967 Arab–Israel war has the Middle East suffered from so many "high intensity" crises. He includes amongst them the continuing slaughter and sectarian conflict in Iraq, the suicide attacks in Afghanistan and the conflict in Gaza. Iran's power, its nuclear pretensions and the potentially dangerous Iran–Syria power nexus with its links to Hamas and Hezbollah are also highlighted, as is the "lower intensity" but no less significant crisis in Lebanon.

To these ongoing crises must be added the more generalized crisis of weakness that afflicts, and has long afflicted, many Arab states. If Iraq is now weak and unstable, it has also generated instability and competition among its neighbors and states further afield, by strengthening radical groups and regimes and weakening status quo and conservative states. This state weakness in turn has contributed to an exacerbation of previously existing problems. It has ramifications for ongoing conflicts and tensions between Israel and Arab states, making them more intractable and less accessible to solutions. Similarly, the Iraq War, its escalation and its consequences have also weakened the capacity and credibility of external actors — whether states or international organizations — to respond effectively to the ongoing challenges to regional and global stability. In some ways the war has stymied the response of such actors, sapping both their resources and their legitimacy.

Not all the "high intensity" conflicts and "lower intensity" crises referred to above are the direct result of the Iraq War, but most are related to it in some way. At the most basic level, then, the Iraq War has increased instability throughout the region. It has not, so far, contributed to a resolution of existing problems, nor has it served as a warning to ambitious regional states; rather, it has introduced a new layer of instability in the region without facilitating resolution of the old. It has produced a series of interrelated changes at the domestic, regional and extra-regional or global level, affecting regimes, peoples, perceptions, conflicts and alliance patterns alike. Iraq has been the focus of change, but the ripple effects have reverberated throughout the region such that few states regionally or globally have been unaffected.

## *Domestic*

At the domestic level, one consequence of the Iraq War for many states has been directly or indirectly to destabilize a number of regimes. It has strengthened radical oppositions — both those that are angered by Western action and those that are inspired by Iraqi resistance — and encouraged sectarianism and jihadism, as reflected in a Sunni–Shi'i divide and widespread transnational support for Iraqi Sunnis. Such tendencies, in turn, have increased regime insecurity and contributed to "de-liberalization" and authoritarian responses. While it would be wrong to regard Middle Eastern regimes as being set on a stable course before the Iraq crisis, there is little doubt that the war has introduced a new layer of regime instability or, put differently, new problems have been superimposed over old ones.

Before 2003, and during the period since the end of the Cold War, the region faced a number of delicate and difficult issues in relation to state and nation building and economic and political development. It was widely acknowledged to be on the periphery of global processes of economic and political liberalization, on the edge of the "Third Wave" of democratization identified by Samuel Huntington, but many would argue that such processes, delicate and fragile as they were, had made some impact and under the right conditions might continue to do so.

The combined effects of 9/11 and the Iraq War have arguably stalled or reversed these processes, revealing their shallow roots. This war, like previous wars, has distracted attention from calls for domestic reform and provided reasons for not undertaking it. The response of regimes to the growth of radical movements and sectarianism has been de-liberalization. So-called moderate regimes in particular have felt threatened by radical Islamic movements and sectarian divides; some have also been implicated in the rise in jihadism. As regimes fear for their stability and survival, the response has been to crackdown on radicalism and restrict political pluralism at home rather than to risk experiments in greater accountability and representation. As in the past, insecurity has been a justification for authoritarianism.

If the Iraq War has slowed the processes of pluralism that saw the rise of Islamic parties and activism, it has also starkly revealed the larger problem of credibility and legitimacy of Arab states, now exacerbated by their positioning on the conflict, their relationship with their own peoples and outside actors. This problem is exemplified in a state like Saudi Arabia — which has been both a source and a target of al-Qaeda activity — and also Egypt and Jordan, all of which are pulled in different directions by competing internal and external pressures. This is not a new phenomenon; indeed it is one that was highlighted 30-odd years ago in an important book by Michael Hudson: *Arab Politics: The Search for Legitimacy*. The fact that it remains such an issue is a testament to how deep-rooted the region's political problems are and how an event like the war in Iraq serves to bring them into sharper relief.

The growth (and schisms) in political Islam and the emergence of a radical front of states and groups, characterized today by the Hamas–Iran–Syria–Hezbollah (HISH) alliance, are also not new phenomena in the Middle East. However, both have been further encouraged and empowered by the consequences of the Iraq War. This development poses an obvious problem for incumbent, more moderate, mainly Sunni regimes, whose dominance has been displaced by the installing of a Shi'i-led government in Iraq, with attendant consequences for their regional and external relations.

## *Intra-regional*

The instability and problems generated at the domestic level are fed and reinforced by instability at the regional level. Here, a particular set of intra-regional problems can be identified.

First, just as the war and its consequences have exacerbated regime weakness, they have also increased regional instability. The greater power and influence of radical national and transnational groups has challenged regimes, state sovereignty and regional institutions, disturbing the prevailing balance of power and the very fabric of the regional system. This also invites intervention — in this sense, both the Israeli interventions in Lebanon in 2006 and in Gaza in 2008–2009, like the US intervention in Iraq itself, were influenced by the perception that radical groups and their state allies had become dangerously strong and that Arab governments had been either complicit in this process or unable to supply an adequate response. Intervention in Iran, by Israel or the United States, following the re-election of the staunchly anti-western President Mahmoud Ahmadinejad, cannot be ruled out.

At another level, the Iraq War has produced problems for the region by exacerbating existing conflicts, contributing to new ones and leading to a changed and volatile balance of power. The new weakness of an important, once pivotal state like Iraq, the wider threat posed to Arab Sunnis or the continuing fragility of Lebanon, have all meant that other states have attempted to exploit the power vacuum. Syria and Iran have been perceived as obvious beneficiaries of the Iraq War; both have used their geographical proximity and links to different religious groups to their advantage. Both have important, though far from identical, stakes in the new Iraqi regime; both have wider aspirations to regional hegemony. Thus, Syria might seek to use its influence in Iraq to help restore its recently lost position in Lebanon, while Iran stands to gain from the consolidation of Shi'i dominance. Indeed, in a recent book, *Iran's Long Reach*, Susan Maloney describes Iran as a "pivotal state in the Muslim world".

A shifting regional balance of power has long been a feature of regional politics, and threats to the prevailing balance from Iran and Syria (among other states) are not new. Further, the relative decline in importance of certain states, like Egypt, and the strengthening of those of the Arabian Gulf, for example, is not a direct result of the Iraq War and is as much about economics as it is about politics. But the regional position of all states has been influenced by the war and the new alignments it has brought about. The particular combination of the Hamas–Iran–Syria–Hezbollah alliance noted above provides a potentially dangerous cocktail from the perspective of Israel, external actors and Arab moderates, as the position of the latter has been weakened and fragmented. This presents an acute problem of regional leadership.

The changing balance of power affects both domestic and international security in many ways. However, it is also wrong to think that Syria and Iran are simple beneficiaries of the current situation. These states are as much competitors as they are allies and both face problems in terms of how to align themselves in the new emerging order. Domestic politics in Iran is fluid and volatile as the post-2009 election crisis demonstrated; the result of Lebanese elections in the same year has also not reopened the door to Syria. So too are there problems for

Israel at the domestic and international level and in terms of measuring the correct response to regional challenges.

If the balance of power has shifted at the political level, this is also reflected by the ripple effects in the regional economy produced by the damaged Iraqi infrastructure and oil production. Though the Iraqi economy is recovering, aided by new international contracts and investment, one effect of its prolonged collapse has been the further empowerment of the wealthy Gulf states.

At the level of regional conflict, outside Iraq, all the region's long-standing conflicts and tensions have been affected in some way, mostly negatively. First, the search for a solution to the Arab–Israel problem and Middle East peacemaking generally were obvious casualties of the Iraq War. Following a Saudi initiative in 2002, which remains on the table, the war has served to further postpone and complicate efforts at any comprehensive settlement by drawing attention and resources elsewhere, while presenting new obstacles in the form of radicalized positions by key actors like Syria, Hamas and Israel and change in balance of forces. The problem, in short, has become more intractable.

Likewise, as regards the Palestine–Israel conflict, Israel's attempts to isolate Gaza with the support of the international community and the acquiescence of at least some Arab states have intensified. The Iraq War has increased radical activity in the region, making Israel feel more insecure. Ultimately, it contributed to a hardening of the Israeli position and intervention in Gaza at the end of 2008, causing widespread destruction and loss of life. The role of potential mediators in both the Palestine–Israel and broader Arab–Israel conflict (whether Saudi Arabia, Egypt or Turkey) has been made more difficult, as has the short-term viability of a two-state solution.

The Israeli invasion of Lebanon in 2006 to suppress Hezbollah and the invasion of Gaza in late 2008/early 2009 with the aim of curbing Hamas activity might not be the direct results of the Iraq War, but the heightening of Israeli insecurity in the light of the strengthening of radical groups following the Iraq invasion has undoubtedly been a factor in influencing Israeli (and Western) politics and the escalation of these conflicts.

Aside from these long-standing regional conflicts, the Iraq War has also contributed to new conflicts within the Arab world, most notably Arab–Arab tensions demonstrated in a sharper Sunni–Shi'i divide, and more recently in divides between different Arab states in relation to their position towards Israel. The destabilizing effect of the jihadi movements in support of Iraq's Sunnis — many neighboring states became conduits for jihadis entering Iraq to support resistance to the Western occupation — and the general increase in activity by radical Islamic groups, has been noted. Another factor of importance for regional states has been the displacement of Iraqis, both internally but also externally. In 2008 there was an estimated two million refugees throughout the region and a slightly higher number of internally displaced Iraqis. The integration and provision for Iraqi refugees and their influence among domestic populations are all potential destabilizing factors.

A related problem, also exacerbated by the conflict and the weakness of key regional actors, has been an ongoing and acute crisis of regional leadership and the parallel inactivity of regional institutions, whether the Arab League or Gulf Cooperation Council, in regards to peace and reconstruction. This, once more, is a reflection of the continuing difficulty of regional states to cooperate and coordinate a common strategy on Iraq and other regional problems, leading to a continuing dependence on outside actors.

Finally, there is the problem of nuclear proliferation. Initially given as a reason for the invasion of Iraq itself, the war has failed to curb the desire of regional actors to acquire weapons of mass destruction. On the contrary, it has made the issue of an Iranian bomb both more contentious, since Iran's power appears to be on the rise, and its acquisition of a nuclear capacity more likely, as efforts at negotiation with the regime in Tehran have failed. It has also raised the nuclear stakes regionally in the sense that Arab states too have started to openly discuss the possibility of acquiring some nuclear capacity.

### *Extra-regional*

The close link between the domestic and regional level problems extends to the international level. Indeed, such is the level of interdependence that domestic and regional level problems are in themselves international problems. While other chapters focus on the problems that the war has posed for global order, this chapter considers the problems that the war has posed for the international relations of the region itself. This war, unlike earlier wars in Afghanistan or the Gulf, for example, was widely unpopular and has weakened the image and credibility of external actors. This has become more acute as early success in war and widespread relief and celebration at the removal of Saddam Hussein have been followed by failure, civil war, the death of thousands of innocent Iraqis, and images of maltreatment of Arab prisoners. Whether active or passive players, all Western powers have been implicated and have lost valuable "soft power" resources as a result.

At another level, the war has led to Western over-extension and inefficient use of resources, a kind of "imperial overstretch" as identified by Paul Kennedy in his work *The Rise and Fall of Great Powers*. This, arguably, has further damaged credibility, drained resources and distracted attention from other pressing problems in the Middle East and elsewhere. In this regard, as noted above, ongoing conflicts like that of Arab–Israel or Palestine–Israel were removed from the forefront of international concerns by the focus of attention on Iraq; this has postponed or crippled international initiatives such as the "Road Map". This problem of neglect was reflected in the last Middle East peace conference at Annapolis in late 2007 where, with attention still focused elsewhere, little substantive progress was made.

The Iraq War has also had an effect on the West's traditional allies within the region, directly or indirectly. In 2003, for example, the United States could not count on the support of Saudi Arabia as had been the case in 2001 over intervention in Afghanistan, or in 1991 in the Gulf War. Unsurprisingly, the Saudis have little affinity with Iraq's Shi'i-led regime. Though some repair of US–Saudi relations has taken place and the two states are engaged in a process of "strategic dialogue", the problems posed by Western policy, and how to respond to it, have revealed new strains. Over the issue of Hamas and divisions within the Palestinian leadership, another state, Jordan, broke ranks with Arab moderates and Western powers to initiate talks with Hamas leaders in 2008.

Finally, and in a related vein, the policies of the US and UK in particular have contributed to problems at other levels, helping to open divides between Arab regimes and Arab peoples, many of whom want to disassociate from the West and its policies, and from their own regimes that continue directly or indirectly to support the West. Rather than providing a model of good governance, the West is identified with military aggression, abuses of power, the killing of civilians, and destruction of infrastructure and cultural heritage. The war has contributed to a changed climate in the Middle East towards outside actors and vice versa, giving wider credence to the idea of a "clash of civilizations" with negative consequences for regional stability and international relations.

The above is reflected in the ongoing popular backlash against the Western powers both inside and outside the Middle East, often expressed through Islamic groups and parties but also in more mainstream political discourse. The Iraq War, in the words of one critical commentator, has come to be seen as yet another example of "the legacy of the Western encounter with the Middle East". This mood blends in more generally with an anti-Western position adopted by a number of developing countries; that of President Hugo Chavez in Venezuela is an example, and is part of a broader global order problem.

## Problems summary

Before considering the further implications and possible remedies of the problems set out above, we briefly conclude this section by reiterating how the Iraq War has aggravated existing domestic, regional and international problems and contributed to new fault lines. One striking feature of the contemporary Middle East system brought sharply into focus by the Iraq War is the interconnectedness of problems; arguably this has always been so, but is a notable aspect of the present crisis in the region. Hence, the Iraq War is linked to the Arab–Israel problem, to the Palestine and Lebanese crises and the nuclear issue; it is also linked to the problems facing states at home and abroad.

Facilitating this interconnectedness are the familiar features of globalization which enable the free flow of information, peoples, ideas, money and arms through ever more sophisticated communications networks. In this regard, the rise of new media — including the popular Al-Jazeera channel and the widespread use of blogs — has had enormous significance throughout the region in mobilizing public opinion and raising regional awareness of current issues.

The Iraq War has provided an opportunity for Arabs to voice their views and make them heard in ways previously impossible. The traumas of the Arab world are thus revealed to both insiders and outsiders, though sympathy for Arab causes is mitigated by a continuing fear of the confrontational nature of radical Islamic groups.

## The Iraq War: Implications

Identifying a set of problems that the Iraq War has generated leads us into a more speculative consideration of the broader implications of the war for the Middle East. Here, two caveats should be noted. First, there is a distinction to be drawn between short and longer term implications; the consequences of the war are still unfolding and its final outcome is unknown. Second, its implications are viewed differently by different groups and actors. The focus here will be on the shorter term implications, which for many are seen as uniformly negative, with some observations included about the longer term picture which suggests a rather different and perhaps more positive outcome.

In a general sense, we may speak of the Iraq War as contributing to a further accumulation of the "lost years" (in one writer's account) in regard to moves to promote peace and stabilize the region at different levels. The Iraq War has had the effect of both stalling and reversing moves towards greater political liberalization and delaying peaceful settlement of regional conflicts, by exacerbating existing tensions and by distracting resources and attention away from other pressing issues.

On a possibly optimistic note, one might argue that in the very long run, the Iraq War and its consequences may come to be regarded not necessarily positively, but as some kind of watershed from which the region has advanced to a more stable future; or that the war, despite its high cost, has become an instrument of positive change. Though this seems unlikely at present, the increased stability in Iraq itself, together with the departure of the Bush administration — arguably the architect of a number of the region's current difficulties — and arrival of a new US administration, whose language at least is very different, provide some grounds for hope.

## Domestic

The domestic level problems identified above — generalized regime instability and reluctance to reform, the growth of sectarianism, challenges from above and below — are unlikely to yield immediate or dramatic changes. Long present in the region, albeit to different degrees, they have been compounded by the Iraq situation and its repercussions are likely to unfold and reverberate for a long time.

As is the case with all major change, however, a period of instability and turmoil may be followed by a reordering, then a period of greater stability. Here it is plausible to ask whether the Iraq War might ultimately give way to a new, more constitutionally-based order? Regime change outside Iraq is certainly likely with continuing turnover of aged incumbents in a number of countries. Successions have already taken place in Syria, Jordan, Saudi Arabia and Morocco and in the leadership of PLO; regime change is also forthcoming in Egypt and Libya (whose leaders have been in power for nearly 30 and 40 years, respectively). If Iraq continues to stabilize politically and economically, there may be pressure on such regimes to increase representation and accountability.

The short-term indicators are not promising: just as likely is that regimes, new and old, will recover their lost footing, and the more authoritarian turn evident since the events of 2003 or even before will allow them to persist in policies initiated in response to Iraq and related events. Given the early reverses and uncertain future of the democratization experiment in Iraq, compounded by the wider failure of the region to make sustained progress towards greater liberalization, the push to further democratize the region in the

Western image is unlikely to take off in the short to medium term. Indeed, the Western experience of liberal democracy and the democratization strategies promoted by the US and its allies have been widely discredited.

The special positions of Israel and Turkey should be noted here. Yet, both states have suffered serious democracy deficits in relation to their own minority populations, with ethnic and religious divides still contradicting democratic imperatives. In addition, neither state provides an obvious or attractive model for the Arab world to follow. Turkey, however, does offer an example of a state where the coexistence of Islam and democracy, within a secular constitution, appears possible.

There are potentially far wider implications for the rise of sectarianism/jihadism. Even if the immediate jihadi threat in Iraq has subsided, it is difficult to see how such movements and their various manifestations will cease to be a threat to regimes in the short term given their widespread appeal. Since they have gained succour from the Iraq War and the responses of Western and Arab regimes, their strength, if temporarily checked, may reappear in different regional contexts. Though a crisis with quite different roots and implications, the events in Gaza, including the heavy-handed Israeli policies and relative inaction by Arab states and outside powers, are likely to reinforce the popularity of such movements rather than provide incentives for greater moderation. In addition, radical movements throughout the region, though very diverse, will continue to receive support from states in whose interests it is to persist in destabilizing policies to enhance their regional position and undermine that of their opponents. Regimes will continue to be pulled in different directions, and responses are likely to remain conservative.

At the economic level, as the restoration of the once shattered Iraqi economy continues, it may become complicated by the effects of the global economic downturn. A generalized economic malaise, with which the region — hitherto shielded by oil rents — is relatively unfamiliar, could further delay any return to political stability.

In sum, domestically at least, the problems identified above have two likely short-term outcomes: continuing radicalism by non-state groups and continuing conservatism by states — effectively the closure of middle roads. This is evident in the de-liberalization of a state like Egypt and in the reaction of moderate Arab states towards political developments in Iraq and the Palestinian territories. Conservatism abroad is likely to be matched by parallel policies at home even if such policies are unpopular. The one avenue not open would appear to be that leading towards greater democratization, accountability and popular participation. Whether or not this is a long-term feature of Middle East politics is hard to predict. Some states may return to a moderate reform agenda if regional stability is ensured. Syria, however, when faced with such a choice, following the succession of Hafez al-Assad by his son Bashar, resisted the path of further liberalization, moving instead towards greater authoritarianism, while what can at best be described as restrictive pluralism prevails in countries like Egypt, Tunisia and Kuwait.

The Lebanese elections of June 2009 tell a somewhat different story following the return of the pro-Western March 14 Alliance, albeit with a still slender majority. If Lebanese politics remains volatile and subject to external influences, for some this represents at least a "moral victory" over Hezbollah and its Syrian allies.

Another country to watch domestically in terms of regime change is Iran, where there are growing divides between the conservative elites in power and the more liberal, reform-minded groups with diverging views of an emerging Iranian polity. Iran's presidential elections in June 2009 were a source of conflict and contestation. Many Iran watchers believe that despite the successful reinstatement of President Ahmadinejad, Iran cannot return to the status quo ante. The Iranian regime has been weakened by the election turmoil and this leaves a question mark over the country's political future and its regional relations, though it would be premature to imagine that the foundations of the Islamic Republic itself are threatened.

Somewhat isolated from the above trends are the smaller Gulf states. Though pro-Western and, for the most part, still deeply conservative, these states form a political and economic "micro-climate" of their own. Here, arguably, the implications of the changes wrought by the Iraq War may be less dramatic at the domestic, regional and international levels. In this way, the war may have helped these states to consolidate their position in any new regional order, though the economic springboard that oil wealth has provided has been affected by the current global crisis which may in turn lead to new political challenges in the region.

## *Intra-regional*

There are necessarily high levels of interdependence between the domestic, regional and international consequences of the Iraq War. The implications of the changed balance of power, with Iraq as a new weak state alongside the already fragile Lebanese state and the divided Palestinian government, are evident in the strength of new regional pretenders. However, even if the Iraq War eventually gives way to a new, more stable balance of power in the longer term, it has increased fragmentation of the region in the short term and contributed to a crisis of regional leadership.

Arguably this crisis of leadership is not new; it is linked to the social, economic and political crises that the region has faced since independence. The region has long been divided between conservative and radical states (as in the Arab Cold War), between oil-haves and have-nots and by ethnic and religious tensions. However, given that these divisions have become more acute and have been aggravated by the Iraq War, they have been brought sharply into focus. The absence of strong regional leadership and regional institutions makes conflict resolution harder and invites external intervention. Indeed, one likely outcome of the Iraq War is that further intervention, in a variety of forms, will continue.

Intervention in Iraq, whether military or non-military, is likely to be prolonged and may continue to generate regional instability and challenges. The possibility of intervention by regional or external powers in the Palestinian territories, Lebanon and Iran cannot be ruled out. For some observers, it is Iran that lies at the heart of a new struggle for the region, with its Shi'i power base, links to radical groups and nuclear program. But this view should be qualified: claims of a new Iranian hegemony are premature. As Arab responses to

Iran's electoral confusion showed, there was quiet satisfaction at the evident challenges to the hardline clerical regime. Iran's position as a radical frontline Shi'i state with widespread cross-regional support cannot be taken for granted. There is no natural Iran–Iraq axis; old rivalries between these states are likely to re-emerge. Therefore, though the regional environment has provided more opportunities for Iran of late, it may be that short-term anxieties about an empowered Iran will give way to a longer term reduction in its perceived threat to the region.

The same may be true for Syria, where again it is wrong to attribute immediate gain to Syria's position post-Iraq War. Its role as a conduit for jihadis entering Iraq and its interest in obstructing the creation of a pro-US Iraq are not in dispute, but Syria also operates in a delicate regional environment where terms like winners and losers are inappropriate. There are gains, but also potential losses from the new fragile balance of power and Syria, like Iran, must accommodate to a shifting local and international framework. As regards the Syria–Iran nexus, the war in Lebanon in 2006 may have brought these countries together as Hezbollah supporters, but the relationship is neither automatic nor necessarily durable. Furthermore, the Lebanese door remains closed to Syria as its political allies have failed to secure electoral victory. Ultimately, Iran and Syria are as much potential competitors as they are allies, operating on different sides of the sectarian divide and with very different interests in Iraq's future.

The regional balance of power has also shifted on a different axis towards the wealthy Gulf states, reflecting a growing economic force and influence that has shielded them from the effects of the war. Oil rents have promoted impressive private sector growth, providing these states with economic leverage and allowing them to become increasingly important regional and global actors, leaving the older established states behind. A widening gap between Arab Gulf states and the rest has thus been opened up by the consequences of the Iraq War. The future, however, is less certain given the finite nature of the region's oil resources, the speculative nature of much Gulf investment and the global economic crisis, which started to hit even the sheltered Gulf emirates by 2008. Now facing economic difficulties, are they likely to press forward as a bloc with a coherent and distinct political agenda? What their future relationship will be with the wider Arab world remains an open question.

Part of the wealthy Gulf group, Saudi Arabia is another state that has been changed by the war. In some ways, the state has been empowered as a regional actor. Though it has faced problems domestically and in its international relations, Saudi Arabia may take on a more important leadership role, as illustrated in its efforts to reinvigorate Arab–Israel peace talks. The Saudis place a high value on regional stability and order and will work towards this goal in regional and global fora. Despite fears of nuclear proliferation, the weakening of Iraq and growth of Shi'i influence, the Saudis do not relish competition with Iran. They have also called for moderation in relation to events in Gaza. Saudi Arabia may have largely overcome its crisis with the US brought about by association with the events of 9/11, but its longer term future remains uncertain in the light of its conservative and aging leadership, imperatives to political and social reforms including the greater emancipation of women, and the general economic downturn.

Another state with a potential regional role to play is Turkey. Turkey remains a pro-Western state and NATO member with EU membership pending. It also acts as a regional balancer, responding to challengers like Syria and Iran. Turkey is a close Iraq watcher, particularly given its concerns about the empowerment of Iraq's Kurds following the war and possible knock-on consequences among its own Kurdish population. Unlike some Arab moderates, Turkey has been increasingly willing to take initiatives on regional crises and offer its services as a peace broker, for example, between Israel and Syria. In short, Turkey continues to emerge as a regional leader and bridge builder.

Aside from this shifting power balance between Arab and non-Arab states, the regional situation will also depend critically on the US–Israel and US–Arab relationships. Both are likely to change as the new US president establishes his position, but the question is how much? The US may restore some regional credibility if it implements a successful exit strategy from Iraq and adopts more regionally sensitive policies.

But the wider damage to regional order remains. Without pressure from the United States, the Israeli position on Palestine is unlikely to substantially change, with the possible result of further empowering its enemies and damaging US credibility.

## Extra-regional

It has often been said that the touchstone of how the Arab world views the West has been the way in which Palestinian grievances are dealt with; to this can now be added how the Iraq War and its consequences are being dealt with. Currently, neither the Palestinian nor the Iraqi crises — nor indeed events in nearby Afghanistan — are good selling points for Western policy. There is always a cost to be borne after externally engineered change, but how high has this cost been for the major actors involved?

Has the war worsened the West–non-West divide? There is a strong argument that the war in Iraq has indeed damaged the US position in the region and globally. This damage has been reinforced by US policy since the war, and most recently during the Israeli intervention in Gaza, where not only the US but Western actors generally have been criticized for inaction and partiality towards Israel in its assault on Gaza. The war and its consequences, as Rick Fawn and Ray Hinnebusch have argued in a recent book, have done serious "reputational" damage.

However, the idea that the Iraq War has permanently or irreversibly damaged the US reputation in the Middle East is mitigated when one considers that the regimes of the Arab Gulf states remain largely pro-Western, and until recently still followed the liberal Washington Consensus economic recipe. Saudi Arabia has arguably recovered from its post-9/11 crisis and remains an important regional ally. Indeed, the challenge to Sunni Arab regimes following the displacement of Sunni hegemony in Iraq means that conservative states like Saudi Arabia are likely to retain a pro-Western axis, even at the risk of popular displeasure over aspects of US policy. The Jordanian case is interesting, however, having "switched" since the Lebanese War of 2006 (when Jordan was applauded for being part of an anti-Hezbollah front) to entering discussions with Hamas, reversing an old pattern of hostility. Nevertheless, this may be interpreted as a pragmatic rather than anti-Western move. Lebanon, for its part, as noted above, has re-elected a pro-Western regime, keeping Syria and its Hezbollah allies out, at least for the time being.

War has revealed the importance of the Iran–Iraq–US triangular relationship, which could yet evolve in a number of different ways. It means, paradoxically, that the US needs Iran, just as it did in the days of the Shah when Iran was seen as an island of stability and friend of the West in a troubled region. US President Obama has spoken of the need to engage with Iran, to "re-set" the US–Iran relationship — a position that is widely shared by many European powers with whom Iran already enjoys important economic relations. It is thus not unreasonable to speculate that the winding down of war with Iraq, together with moves to settling the nuclear impasse, could lead, after many stalled efforts by both sides, to a general improvement in relations. The US has repeatedly misread the Iranian position in the past; for example, after 9/11 when Iran was identified as part of an "axis of evil". Iran is without doubt a far more complex and nuanced polity than any simple black and white version allows. This means that some moderate realignment towards the West is certainly possible.

In a wider sense, however, continuing fear and dislike of US action in the region — assisted by a proliferation of new media outlets — at the level of public opinion will take time to reverse, and here Obama's diplomatic abilities and negotiating skills will be put to the test. Indeed, in contemplating the longer term international implications of the war for the region, much will depend on the new US administration and its actions. Whether Obama can initiate a policy substantially different from his predecessor and therefore reshape relations is too early to say; if the initial signs were positive, many remain sceptical. It is not only against the handling of the Iraq crisis and its consequences that the US and its allies will be judged. There has also been considerable discussion about Obama's ability to bring Israel and the Palestinians to the negotiating table. Some Arabs are already disappointed that Obama has not displayed a firmer hand in dealing with the Israelis, whether on the issue of settlements or a future Palestinian state.

## Remedies

It is often said that "home-grown" solutions are best, or that local and regional problems are best solved at the local level. But this aspiration has hitherto proved elusive in the Middle East. There are not, as yet, signs of any burgeoning Arab consensus, or a renaissance of Arab (or Islamic) institutions in the service of peace. However, it is wrong to write off Arab or indeed non-Arab regimes and institutions and imagine that a solution lies only in the hands of the West. Certain states have attempted regional mediation roles including Saudi Arabia, Turkey and Egypt, and it is likely that major regional and cross-regional institutions (e.g., the League of Arab States, the Gulf Cooperation Council, the Organization of the Islamic Conference) will also become involved in reconstruction efforts in Iraq and in wider peacemaking processes. These, alongside other multilateral initiatives, should be encouraged. In particular, a more inclusive regional institution which incorporates a wider array of actors, Arab and non-Arab, would provide a useful starting point for regional negotiations.

### Domestic

Any efforts to remedy the wider problems caused by the Iraq War will need to focus squarely on the domestic level. Arguably, domestic politics provides both the source and the solution to the region's difficulties.

First, given that domestic order — comprising political, social and economic arrangements — has a close link with regional and international order, it is clear that states and regimes will need to reform to take greater responsibility for their region. At present, domestic arrangements in many states are not such that a plurality of voices and opinions are being heard. Regimes have chosen to crack down on opposition or to silence radical groups rather than seeking methods of engagement. This has widened the gap between incumbent regimes and radical groups and also between regimes and populations. In an age where public opinion cannot be readily suppressed, it is important that regimes take steps to allow greater representation and voice. Peoples across the region, writes Richard Norton, author of *Hezbollah*, want better government, even if they are not sure as to what type of government this should be. Political reform of some kind will certainly be part of any regional solution.

## *Intra-regional*

All regimes ultimately share an interest in stability and order, and this may provide a way forward for concerted regional responses that hitherto have been lacking.

The new balance of power has produced new regional actors who need to be included, not excluded, from any settlement. Regional leadership is urgently required, but it remains unclear which state or states are willing to supply it. Turkey, Egypt and Saudi Arabia have all shown greater assertiveness and played some roles in regional containment and mediation. Jordan is a rare example of a state that has actively involved itself in post-conflict institution building, by helping to reconstruct the Iraqi police. Under the Neighboring Countries Initiative, an expanding group of regional states now meet regularly in an attempt to contain the effects of the Iraq War and rebuild confidence. However, given that regional states have such high stakes in any emerging order, much more could be done.

Reflecting the absence of regional leadership, formal institutions in the Middle East have been notoriously weak and have failed to tackle regional problems effectively. They are cumbersome, slow to act, and reveal divisions and lack of commitment among core members. There is no pan-Middle Eastern institution. Typically, non-Arab states like Iran or Israel have been excluded from formal regional arrangements, though Iran has actively promoted cooperative and bilateral initiatives within its immediate neighborhood. In a world where regional institutions are taking on more important roles (whether in Europe, Africa or Latin America), there is every reason to believe that they could also become more important actors in the

Middle East. Existing institutions like the Arab League and the Gulf Cooperation Council could play more significant roles in supplementing the informal initiatives described above.

It may be the case that such regional initiatives cannot fully substitute for the role of external states or ultimately an institution like the United Nations in restoring regional order. However, there are obvious advantages to local action, not least in that it may enjoy greater legitimacy. There is a tendency among Western powers to critique the role that regional powers play or to despair of Arab willingness to act, but there is also a need to appreciate the constraints and limitations on Arab leaders, and ensure that their broader concerns are incorporated into future settlement proposals.

### *Extra-regional*

The evident limitations to regional-level action, reflecting the lack of capacity and autonomy in the face of serious internal and external pressures, mean that remedies will continue to be externally driven. Even if unpalatable to some actors, it is likely that the United States will remain a major player. Certainly, as regards the Middle East peacemaking in the past, the US has been a key actor in bringing the different sides together. Indeed, US scholar Joseph Nye has suggested that the US is the *only* power able to bring together mutual enemies.

If this interpretation seems to accord too much importance to the US role, we should remember that power (understood as the ability to influence outcomes) requires both the different resources — political, economic, military and ideological — that power comprises, as well as the willingness to use them. And here, when we consider the other options — whether internal or external to the region — there is a serious shortfall, if not in resources, then in the capacity and willingness to use them effectively and wisely.

It is undoubtedly the case that both Russia and China today are significant regional players. But despite their economic and strategic interests in the Middle East, neither (notwithstanding Russia's participation in the Middle East Quartet) has demonstrated an immediate desire to become seriously involved in helping to promote solutions to regional conflicts. In the short term, at least, they do not appear to be plausible problem solvers as has been demonstrated with regard to Iran's nuclear capacity, the Darfur question, or wider Middle East peacemaking issues.

Europe, on the other hand, in the form of the EU, has frequently been cast and has cast itself as a power with both the capacity and the willingness to influence the Middle Eastern political scene at a variety of levels. However, despite much talk about its possible roles, outside the economic arena at least, the EU's attempts to strike a different posture from that of the US or to make an impact on regional conflicts have been limited. Europe has neither effectively counterbalanced the US, nor has it fulfilled the soft power roles suggested by some commentators. An effective common foreign and security policy has remained elusive, revealing the divides within Europe itself. However, if there is little reason to suppose that the EU will become a major actor in any future political settlement in the Middle East (or "a player not a payer" as Ariel Sharon once mocked), there is clearly a potential role for the EU to play in framing an effective international response. It has demonstrated, for example, a sustained commitment for a two-state solution to the Israel–Palestine issue. The EU has large resources and important trade and other links with Israel, the Palestinians and Iran; it has demonstrable institution building capacity. It also has the potential, through EU example and aid, to convert itself into a more convincing ally in the search for order in the Middle East.

Outside the EU, there is of course a significant role to be played by other international institutions, notably the United Nations, and other multilateral and non-governmental bodies in rebuilding Iraq and promoting regional order. The questionable legitimacy of the Iraq invasion limited the UN's early roles, but these have expanded in the extended peace building and reconstruction phase, through the activities of the UN Assistance Mission for Iraq (UNAMI). The UN has a long history of involvement in Middle East conflict prevention and peace processes — historically, the Middle East is the region to which the most international sanctions have been applied. It is impossible to imagine a future regional order "beyond Iraq" in which the United Nations and its different agencies will not play a major role. UN initiatives like the "Alliance of Civilizations", established in 2005, point to further possible avenues of addressing the wider issues arising from the Iraq War and other regional conflicts.

More generally, the international community needs to strive for an even-handed and regionally sensitive approach, whilst assuming greater responsibility for the troubles of the Middle East. Rather than exploiting US difficulties in Iraq, Gaza and elsewhere, it should recognize that instability is contrary to the interests of all and encourage genuine multilateral cooperation and collective action, perhaps by building on some of the successful experiences of the early 1990s. Both the United States and Europe have launched and relaunched different cooperative initiatives — the Greater Middle Eastern Partnership and European Neighborhood Policy are two examples, yet neither have yielded the desired outcomes. One problem may be, to return to an argument put forward at the start of this chapter, that Western perceptions of regional order, which today incorporate the idea of a "greater Middle East", simply do not map on to local realities. Hence, the importance of working with local actors and institutions in the search for long-term solutions.

All the remedies suggested above are subject to huge limitations. One thing is clear, however: regional order in the Middle East will not depend solely on the actions of any single state or group of states. The US will have to share its position with both emerging regional powers and other external actors and institutions. This outcome is in any case more likely in the new Obama administration, which has highlighted a renewed commitment to US allies and support for multilateralism. This, alongside the improved security situation in Iraq itself, may ease the way forward for staged troop withdrawals and reconstruction of regional order engaging a wider array of international actors.

## Conclusion: Towards a New Regional Order in the Middle East?

The inauguration of President Obama in January 2009 with a "new look" Middle East policy gave rise to hopes for a different approach to the problem of order in the Middle East. The region was quickly placed at the forefront of Obama's foreign policy agenda when he announced closure of the Guantanamo Bay facility, and his intention to seek dialogue with Iran and to advance withdrawal of forces from Iraq. His speech at Cairo University in June 2009, where he spoke of "a new beginning for US–Muslim relations", reiterated these intentions. These were positive signs. However, beyond presidential rhetoric, a lot more remains to be done in rebuilding relations with the Arab world in particular, and here the Palestine issue, as much as Iraq, may prove once more to be the ultimate test.

As the first decade of the 21st century draws to a close, it can be concluded that the experience of war in Iraq has been uniformly detrimental to regional order. This is particularly apparent when one considers the objectives of that war from the perspective of Western states. Whether or not anything more positive emerges in the years "beyond Iraq" remains to be seen. One thing seems clear, however: the Iraq War has not provided the basis for a more stable order in the short to medium term. It has generated hostility and mistrust, increased conflict, and helped to delay painful decisions about political liberalization and economic restructuring. Western powers will surely be more cautious in engaging in further acts of regional intervention which not only fail to advance their own interests but provoke further resistance.

To regard the Iraq War, however, as exposing "a new struggle for the Middle East" — one which sees Israel, the US and its allies pitted against the forces of Islamic extremism supported by Syria and Iran — is a simple and dangerous generalization. Iran is a complex polity and a state with which negotiations are certainly possible, despite the hawkish language of the Ahmadinejad administration. It is ultimately informed by pragmatic considerations — like most states — and is an unlikely leader of a rejectionist front of Arab states and non-state groups against the Western powers. Here it is important to distinguish rhetoric from reality. All regional powers wish to promote their own interests and have different visions of what a desirable order might look like, but stability is a common goal.

If the Iraq War becomes a watershed, forming a plateau from which domestic, regional and international actors can advance and gain improved understanding of the complexities of the region's peoples and conflicts and move beyond fear, misperception and narrow self-interest, history may judge it somewhat differently. There are many useful lessons that can be learned from the past. Perhaps the most important and immediate one that stands out from the Iraq War is that attempts by Western powers to mould the Middle East according to their own prescribed visions of order have been built on sand.

Chapter 3

# Just Another Liberal War? Western Interventionism and the Iraq War

Nicholas Kitchen and Michael Cox

## Introduction

The tragedy in Iraq set within the context of the crisis unfolding in the greater Middle East forces us to seek an answer to a question that many have already asked, but few have so far answered successfully: namely, what led those who set out with such high hopes to liberate one country whilst forcing the pace of reform in many others to the decision to go to war against Saddam Hussein's Baa'th regime? It was hardly as if the war was forced upon them, or that the key individuals were unaware of the huge risks involved. Nor were they ignorant of the fact that the decision flew in the face of much expert advice and a great swathe of international public opinion. Still, they went ahead, some willingly, others less so, with consequences that most (even those who supported the original decision) now agree have done more to weaken the United States in the international system than strengthen it. Indeed, even Americans with impeccable establishment credentials now accept that the war has proven catastrophic, undermining America's soft power appeal in several countries and causing immense damage to the international order more generally — damage that will take several years to repair, if of course it can ever be repaired at all.

Several accounts now exist of the complicated course of events that led George W. Bush, in close association with Tony Blair, to translate the war on terror into a war against a regime that had nothing to do with the original attack on the United States in 2001. These range across the board from those who stress the almost tragic combination of contingency, miscalculation and the disturbing impact of unforeseen events on the policy process; to those who focus, in different degrees, on the malevolent influence of the neo-cons, the oil industry, the Israel lobby, and of course the powerful political alliance forged between the Vice President and the Secretary of Defence within an administration led by a man whose moral view of the world strongly inclined him to take action against a regime that had been left in place by none other than his presidential father back in 1991. All wars, it seems, have the power to divide those who later seek to uncover its deeper causes. However, few wars in recent times have divided policymakers and scholars alike as much as the Iraq War. Nor is there much chance that this divide will be overcome anytime soon. The scale of the tragedy in Iraq itself, the radicalizing impact of the occupation on a younger generation of Muslims worldwide and the obvious damage Iraq has done to the legitimacy of Western, and in particular American, claims of international leadership all seem certain to have significant international consequences for decades.

Thus, America's intervention in Iraq is destined to become the key historical event in the region, in American foreign policy and in broader discussions of international relations. Like Munich and Vietnam before it, the "lessons" of Iraq will be "learnt" and cited by policymakers. That we should beware historians bearing false analogies is not in doubt; but nor should we be under any illusions that parallels will be drawn with and conclusions derived from the Iraq War far into the future of international politics. Yet despite the huge body of material claiming to uncover the "real" reasons behind this war of choice, one element has been largely missing from the debate — the extent to which liberal ideas constituted both the moral and intellectual climate within which Iraq policy was conceived, and provided the historical analogues for the invasion. The fact that debate concerning this liberal *zeitgeist* has been largely absent has meant that despite the rush to draw conclusions from the conflict, the content of liberal ideas has remained uninterrogated. With all the conspiracy-theory driven excitement about the roles of shadowy "neo-cons" and notions of an imperial war for oil, scholarship has largely skipped over the extent to which the Iraq War represents the logical fulfilment — and the grand test case — of a deeply rooted set of liberal ideas that flourish in the optimism of the post-Cold War period and which reject realist caution and place notions of ethics, universal rights and conditionality of sovereignty at the heart of Western foreign policy.

Few wars are controversial before they are fought. Yet the United States' stated policy of regime change in Iraq split the Western alliance and brought, according to the estimates of French political scientist Dominique Reynié, some 36 million people around the world out onto the streets in the months leading up to the invasion. For arguably the first time, the United States experienced genuinely global popular resistance to its hegemony, which the rest of the world had, up to that point, generally regarded as relatively benign. Far from just discontent over a particular policy, the level of controversy over Iraq represented a litmus test of the American Empire, a referendum on whether the 21st century would be American too.

Claiming a "coalition of the willing" numbering 49 (and including such international big-hitters as Palau and Tonga), the United States, together with the UK, Poland and Denmark — the only coalition members whose support extended to providing troops — invaded Iraq regardless and succeeded in removing Saddam Hussein from power. Yet "Old Europe" led by France and Germany, China, Russia, Latin America's major powers and even Israel remained on the sidelines, unwilling to give their assent to America's choice. As the quick, clean victory of the invasion gave way to messy defeat in a fractured state ridden by insurgency, notions of American decline resurfaced. The unipolar moment was over, and in its place were scattered the ashes of what Michael Mann called "the first failed empire of the 21st century."

Why did the United States make a choice that appeared even in advance to be likely to have such counterproductive effects to its own standing in the world? The official rationale is more difficult to discern than one might expect. The United States cited UN Resolutions 678 and 687 to authorize the invasion, which allowed for the use of all necessary measures to compel Iraq to comply with its international obligations. Those obligations had their roots in the 1991 Gulf War and were designed to keep Saddam "in his box," but their use in authorizing the conflict was little more than legalese. Despite the efforts of the United Kingdom to keep a sceptical American administration working through the United Nations, the UN Security Council had refused to sanction an invasion in the belief that even if containment of the Iraqi regime was not working, then at least the UN should spend more time establishing that fact and provide Iraq with more opportunity to comply with the demands of the international community.

Yet the resolutions of the early 1990s do reflect the dominant nature of the official discourse in the United States in 2002 and 2003, namely that Iraq was not contained, that it had continued to develop weapons of mass destruction (WMDs) and that it posed a threat to its neighbors and to international security more generally. This was the argument that Colin Powell presented to the United Nations in his dramatic — and now much derided — presentation in February 2003. Yet as Paul Wolfowitz noted in an interview with *Vanity Fair* that May, WMDs were chosen for bureaucratic purposes as "the one reason that everyone could agree upon." This admission confirmed the sense of many both inside and outside the policymaking process that the real motivation for the conflict lay elsewhere.

Having said that, the argument of WMDs should not be dismissed out of hand. The failure to find WMDs in Iraq was an embarrassing and worrying intelligence failure, the causes of which have been documented elsewhere (notably by Robert Jervis), but it should be remembered that in 2002 the Western intelligence agencies were in agreement that Saddam Hussein had in all likelihood continued to develop WMD capacity in the years following the Gulf War. The division was between those states favoring a US-led war predicated on the notion that only regime change could address the WMD issue and those who thought inspections could be made to work.

The argument for war due to the presence of WMDs in Iraq rests on two related propositions. The first is that the events of 9/11 redefined the risks to Western societies of WMD proliferation, because the nihilistic nature of suicide terrorism renders deterrence redundant. Rogue states, opposed to the interests of the United States and in possession of WMDs, can therefore directly threaten the United States itself by proxying with fundamentalist Islamist groups. That 9/11 was crucial to Iraq policy can be seen in the speeches of Bush and Blair — who declared respectively that "after September 11th, the doctrine of containment just doesn't hold any water" because it would only be a matter of time before terrorism and weapons of mass destruction, "two sides of the same coin," come together. Whilst the intelligence services were unable to corroborate allegations of links between Saddam Hussein and al-Qaeda, the possibility of such links, continually floated by the Bush administration, took hold with the American public to the extent that soon after the invasion, a *Washington Post* poll found that 69% believed Saddam to have been personally involved in the September 11th attacks. That the encouragement of such beliefs among the American public bolstered the administration's case is not in doubt, but the deeper reasoning that underlay the need to wage war on Iraq was that 9/11 changed the rules of the game: regimes hostile to the United States that develop weapons of mass destruction can no longer be contained because of the possibility that they will supply capabilities to terrorist groups who cannot be deterred from using them. Indeed, the failed logic of deterrence theory in this new security environment requires that threats are pre-empted, because by the time a hostile state has achieved WMD capacity there is no means of preventing their passing that capacity to terrorist groups such as al-Qaeda.

We can see the impact of 9/11 very clearly in the processes of American planning itself. As late as August 2001, a paper presented to policymakers spoke in terms of pressuring Saddam rather than ousting him; but in the hours and days after 9/11, Secretary of Defense Donald Rumsfeld was asking for plans for the removal of the Iraqi dictator. 9/11 thus provided both the shift in perception of threat and the opportunity to, as Blair put it, "reorder this world around us."

At the heart of Blair's "world" is, of course, the broader Middle East. The second argument from WMDs is that the United States has an interest in the stability of that region, and that were Iraq to obtain significant WMD capacity, the balance of power in the Middle East would be altered in a deeply unsettling way, particularly in relation to the security of Iraq's neighbors. That meant the political security of Israel (the keystone democracy in the region) and the resource security of the major oil producers — Iran, Kuwait and Saudi Arabia. Saddam had shown himself to be aggressive and unpredictable, and the destabilizing effects of an arms race or interstate war triggered by Iraqi WMD capacity were a very real threat to Western interests.

It is these strategic interests in the Middle East that provide the case of Iraq with its own particular resonance and urgency, which the WMD-seeking activities of North Korea, for example, do not warrant. America's relations with the Middle East (and Britain's before that) have historically revolved around the two key interests of support for the state of Israel and access to a regular supply of well-priced oil. It is therefore unsurprising that these key interests formed the central tenets of more conspiratorial explanations for the invasion. From the left, explanations abounded that the economic logic of oil was the central factor in the decision to oust Saddam Hussein. At the same time, commentators pointed to the links between administration officials and Israel's Likud Party, in particular a strategy document from the mid-1990s entitled "A Clean Break" that advocated regime change in Iraq as part of a newly aggressive Israeli strategic approach.

Such explanations tended to focus their analysis on a shadowy "cabal" of so-called neo-conservative ideologues at the heart of the Bush administration. The conspiracy-theory story of Zionists and US imperialists linked to "big oil" is well-known, and there is no doubt that there were members of the administration who saw the events of 9/11 as their Pearl Harbor, i.e., providing the opportunity to put in place a policy of lasting American hegemony based on military might. And for many of those individuals, the place to start — for material, historical and ideological reasons — was Saddam Hussein's Iraq. After all, as the President noted, "this is the guy who tried to kill my dad."

George H.W. Bush wasn't the only person that Saddam had tried to kill, and on most other occasions his attempts had met with greater success. A corollary argument that was made in parallel with issues of security throughout the debate over the invasion derived from human rights. Saddam ran a particularly unpleasant domestic security apparatus that utilized torture and mass executions, had ruthlessly put down the Shiite uprising in the aftermath of the first Gulf War, and had used chemical weapons against Iraq's Kurds. Here was a monstrous dictator, and the world had a moral duty to the people of Iraq to rid them of his regime. As two prominent neo-conservatives put it in the title of their book, "Saddam's Tyranny" was "America's Mission."

The replacement for that regime would be a liberal democracy, as America pledged to undertake an act of state-building not seen since the end of WWII. Indeed, the successes of the cases of Germany and Japan were regularly cited by supporters of the invasion. So a second corollary to the argument that Saddam represented a threat was the notion that his removal and replacement with a modern, prosperous democratic Arab state would serve as a stabilizing and pacific force in the region. Not only would Israel's security be enhanced by the presence of a democratic neighbor, but a democratic Iraq would reduce Western dependence on Saudi Arabia, an increasingly problematic alliance due to that country's human rights record and because 15 of the 19 hijackers during 9/11 were Saudi.

What this rather muddled mix of grounds, justifications and explanations suggests is that no one factor really represents a sufficient cause for the invasion of Iraq in 2003, which fits with Wolfowitz's statement that WMDs were selected as *the* "reason" for purposes of presentation and bureaucratic efficiency. Supporters of the war did so for a diverse range of reasons — some interest-based, others ideological. This does not necessarily mean that the war was unjustified — a cumulative case could be regarded as sufficient, although the sum of bad ideas hardly constitutes a good idea. Yet the aspect that has been largely missing from both the analysis of the decision to go to war and the resultant critiques is the extent to which all of these diverse rationales were assessed within an intellectual framework which reinforced their individual and cumulative merit, an intellectual framework that is so pervasive in Western societies that it represents an almost non-falsifiable *zeitgeist*.

## The Liberal Zeitgeist

Iraq represents the high watermark of a Western approach to international security that has dominated since the end of the First World War. From liberalism arose the unchallenged ideology of modernity — the final victor at the end of history, its logic confirmed by the end of the Cold War, and the sole lens through which to view international politics. In what follows we will discuss those assumptions and trace the progress of Western thinking about legitimacy and force in international relations, thinking which reached its logical conclusion in the 2003 Iraq invasion.

Historically, when thinking about international politics, liberals have made the state the logical analogue of the person in liberal political theory. States therefore have the right of self-determination, which confers a responsibility on other states to not interfere in the internal governance of that state. By granting states rights of their own, that state's citizens have their liberties protected from the intrusions of external actors; individuals' liberty is therefore dependent on the liberty of the state.

Such liberal thought is most famously demonstrated by Woodrow Wilson's 14 points and constituted the ideological scaffolding of the American-led effort to dismantle the European powers' colonial empires after World War II. Individuals had rights, therefore groups of individuals could aggregate the rights of their members, and so states, as the representatives of their peoples, derived from them the right to govern, free from the exploitation of dominant colonial powers. The success in rebuilding the defeated Axis powers into responsible members of the international community fuelled a belief in the socially transformative powers of liberal politics, and as the Cold War emerged from the rubble of post-war Europe to pit nations against each other in bipolar ideological conflict, the United States evoked the principles of sovereignty, self-determination and the liberties of peoples again and again in its fight against the "Evil Empire" of the Soviet Union and communism's soul-sapping collectivism.

At the same time, liberalism's international thought has a deeper corollary to the inviobility of the individual, the principle from which the rights of states derive. For Locke, a person's liberty is based upon the "property in his own person," that is, the idea that humans are naturally pre-contractual beings. Locke sees the logical progression of this basic idea as being the force that drove modernization from one's own subsistence labor to bartering; from bartering to money; from money to land ownership; and from land ownership to states. In this understanding, political liberalism and capitalism are more than just mutually constituted, they are logically inseparable. Capitalism both relies upon the individual's freedom to pursue his own happiness and legitimizes that quest. The moral imperative of human freedom, it turns out, is an economic imperative too.

Liberalism's basic commitment to private property drove one side of the ideological conflict of economies that was the Cold War, and nowhere is the dedication to a Lockean conception of labor and capital more socially embedded than in the United States and its uniquely American Dream. Here capitalism is an entire way of life, or as one author put it, "a pervasive, quasi-religious entity." So it is unsurprising that the American liberal thought as applied to international politics has always had distinctly economic undertones. Modernization in the international context became synonymous with progress towards liberalism, which all meant development — spreading economic growth defined as income per capita. This thinking was spectacularly vindicated by the peaceful surrender of Communism and the end of the Cold War: a victory earned by the socio-economic system that bought free citizens washing machines and home computers over the collectivism that brought a bound society queues, famine and injustice.

With the collapse of the Soviet Union it was thought that the universal availability of capitalist prosperity would lead inexorably to stability, peace and the dominance of those liberal values of self-determination and non-interference that were so inseparable from the economic doctrine. Yet the history of the Cold War did not really support such an optimistic conclusion. Far from economic liberalism going hand-in-hand with liberal politics, the United States was forced on several occasions to choose between unelected modernizing elites and democratic governments with less pro-capitalist sentiments, and had tended to back the capitalists. Realists would not have expected any different, of course, but the peaceful end of the Cold War had plunged realism into a crisis of confidence, and the new world order had promised that such unpalatable compromising of liberal principles would be a thing of the past. With the shackles of the Cold War's overriding imperatives thrown off, liberal internationalism could not only be true to its principles, it could do so with the backing of the world's unassailable superpower, which could harness its unipolar moment to establish an enduring liberal peace. The American revolution could be made universal.

Across the Atlantic, however, European liberalism had traditionally differed from its American counterpart, in particular in its attitude towards the use of force. European liberalism was distinctive in that it had arisen out of two European wars, and was therefore focused on the creation of peace rather than moral notions of justice. Instead of strongly advocating a particular form of socio-economic organization predicated on limited government as in the American liberal model, liberalism in the European context revolved around institutional arrangements designed to maintain stability and resolve international disputes through peaceful means, hence the drive for European institutional integration following the potentially destabilizing end of communist rule in Eastern Europe. That process having proceeded more smoothly than anyone had anticipated, by the end of the 1990s a shift in European thought at the domestic level began to bring European liberalism more into line with its revolutionary American counterpart.

This move, termed the "Third Way" and often dismissed as nothing more than cynical political positioning, actually represented a genuine shift in liberal orthodoxy. In European states where safety-net welfare states were far more central to societal organization than in the United States, liberals began to speak of the notion that individuals' rights conferred particular responsibilities. Particularly strong in Britain and Germany, the Third Way amounted to a redefinition of the social contract between the citizen and the state, which would now be one where the citizen's rights are conditional on certain responsibilities in terms of conduct: not duties imposed from outside, but the voluntary assumption of commitments to particular liberal values and the expectation of such responsible behavior.

The Third Way politics of Blair and Schroeder in the 1990s coincided with the American conception in international politics that the rights of states were conditional on certain behavioral responsibilities. In this way, liberals throughout the West came to advocate a "rehierarchization" of international relations, one that would imbue democratic states with particular rights of governance. In particular, democratic states should have the right to intervene, militarily if need be, in order to protect the rights of individuals within other states where those rights were being violated by their government.

The Cold War had served to establish not only American engagement with the world but also the ideological rhetoric — both in public and in private — in terms of which that engagement would take place, a rhetoric that emphasized the universal nature of American values. In the 1990s, that rhetoric of liberal values was harnessed as a vital source of legitimacy and justification by Western governments. Indeed, international law evolved to allow developed countries to conduct policing measures — involving the use of military force and the violation of norms of sovereignty — in cooperative actions to deal with civil wars and vicious regimes. This was a new doctrine of international community, said Tony Blair in Chicago in 1999, but fundamentally it rested on one very clear fact: the military dominance of the United States. The revolution in military affairs had given the United States — the source of 50% of world defense spending — a military capacity so advanced that it could conduct "virtual" wars using air power and precision bombing that could target despots whilst causing only minimal "collateral damage," and at almost zero risk to American service personnel.

This new activism on the part of Western liberal states reflected a belief that politically liberal states were domestically and internationally peaceful states. Deriving from Kant and bolstered by empirical evidence that suggested that liberal states do not go to war with each other, liberals tied the embedding standards of individual liberty and the precepts of market democracy to the creation of a stable, peaceful international order. This faith in the "liberal peace" was a cornerstone assumption of American foreign policy in the post-Cold War period, epitomized in the Clinton strategy of "enlargement" of the community of market democracies.

Yet during the 1990s, despite these US-led policies to open markets and the near-universalization of liberal economic theory, the assumption that capitalism and liberal democracy would go hand-in-hand was thrown into sharp relief. The United States undertook military interventions in defense of a range of liberal political principles in Kuwait, Somalia, Haiti, Bosnia and Kosovo. As Freedman notes, the consequences of passivity in Rwanda in 1994 and Srebrenica the following year having weighed heavily on liberal consciences, increasingly Europe too came to advocate the need to use force to address the mismanagement of other states' internal affairs.

Liberalism had therefore come to view non-democratic states as obstacles to a peaceful international system, and liberals advocated policies to spread democratic values that ranged from simple example to democracy promotion by means of trade and foreign aid, right up to military intervention and nation-building. States that did not respect the liberties of their own people could not be relied upon to respect the sovereign liberties of other states — either their political liberty or the liberty of their capital in a globalized economy. Sovereignty, in liberal thought, was no longer the absolute right of a state — it would be conditional upon the political character of that state.

Yet the question of who would make the judgment of a state's political character was soon a source of tension between Western liberals. At the same time that Europe was beginning to embrace American interventionism based on the liberal values of the international community, America's relationship with that community was deteriorating. A major ideological shift in American politics had been underway since the 1970s, a shift that rejected the European-style liberalism of Lyndon Johnson's Great Society reforms at home in favor of an American nationalism abroad. Here was a new Americanism, notable for an ideological belief that treaty commitments were by definition constraints which represented a privation of the liberty of the United States and therefore of its citizens. This United States would act for the high rhetoric of its liberal values, but it would do so on its own terms — it was, after all, the indispensible nation.

In this sense, the transatlantic split over Iraq was foreshadowed by the growing schism between American and European liberalisms, a division laid bare by Robert Kagan's *Paradise and Power*. The European critique is that the United States abandoned liberalism, that the neo-conservatives were far-right imperialists that bore very little resemblance to liberals. This case has also been made by some Americans, Tony Smith accusing those liberals who supported the Iraq invasion of having made a "pact with the devil."

Essentially this critique is one of means rather than ends, yet on closer inspection it is difficult to see where the substantive ideological difference lies. It is often claimed that in waging war on Iraq, the United States defied the United Nations, and that the war was therefore illegal. Yet just a few years earlier, Western liberals had been largely united in support of intervention in Kosovo — an action undertaken without UN authorization. Liberal attitudes towards legality had been blurred during the 1990s, when scholars began to argue that the moral asymmetry between liberal and illiberal societies translates liberal ideas of legitimacy into ideas of legality. And it was not just American neo-conservatives, but European liberals too, who were prepared to argue for the "laws of the jungle" when dealing with illiberal states, with the British diplomat Robert Cooper speaking approvingly of liberal imperialism as a force for peace and order.

There is a second flipside to the legality argument. Whilst in 2004 Kofi Annan labelled the Iraq invasion illegal, it seems unlikely he would have reached such a conclusion had the war been successful. Indeed, the Secretary-General had previously seen the timely but legally ambiguous interventions in Kosovo and East Timor as justifiable when states were unable to prevent death and suffering being inflicted on their own populations. The ultimate outcome of the dominance of liberal thought is not simply that liberal equals legal, but that where liberalism's preferred sources of legitimacy cannot be obtained, then legitimacy, even legality, may be conferred by the combination of liberal motivations and success.

Liberalism as applied to issues of international politics had therefore ended up in a slightly counter-intuitive place by 2003. The progress of liberal international thought — from sovereignty to human security, from prioritizing peace to prioritizing justice — had been a reflection of its overwhelming dominance of the ideological landscape. With no serious competitor in the realm of ideas, liberalism defined the boundaries of debate and provided the lens through which to view international politics. The maxims of this *zeitgeist* are simple, and this simplicity exerts a logical force that is compelling. Liberalism tells us that people have rights and so do states. It tells us that people's rights are prior to those of states. It tells us that legitimacy matters in international politics. It tells us that legitimacy is conferred by liberal credentials. It tells us that interventions are justifiable in defense of people's rights. Thus, liberalism's precepts were the unchallenged arbiter of the ethics of the Iraq conflict: issues of practicality and policy aside, liberal thought by 2003 assumed that the rights of the Iraqi people merited intervention on their behalf, that failure to do so would damage the legitimacy of Western actors, and that success in Iraq would reinforce the legitimacy, even the legality, of the action itself.

Yet, taken together to their logical conclusion, the maxims of the liberal *zeitgeist* produce an outcome that is profoundly counter-intuitive to the principles themselves — that Western powers would invade and occupy a sovereign state, preemptive of a just cause, and free a people who had shown only limited desire to be so liberated. In the post-Cold War liberal *zeitgeist*, questions of national interest and realist restraint were only ever secondary to the ethical imperatives of liberal order. Any questions of feasibility could be answered by the overwhelming dominance of US military power. In essence, for the United States and the international community that sought to involve the United States, anything that could be justified in liberal terms went. There was simply no other way of looking at problems of international politics.

The Iraq War was a war waged against a destabilizing, threatening and illiberal state; a war to bring human rights and the benefits of market democracy to an oppressed people and the first domino in the extension of the liberal peace to the broader Middle East. Yet it split the Western liberal community. Why?

## A Liberal Split?

Liberal dissatisfaction with the Iraq War on both sides of the Atlantic is somewhat perplexing given the history of liberal internationalist thought. Yes, the bypassing of the international institutional framework was far from ideal, and yes, the war was probably contrary to international law. But few liberals had seen these as definitive bulwarks in the past, particularly when there were human security concerns at stake, as there certainly were in Iraq. Indeed, in its scale and profile, the Iraq War had the potential to establish new norms of progressive liberal engagement whereby the autocrats of Moscow and Beijing could no longer cast a veto on the rights of the world's oppressed peoples. In this sense, it was a grand test case of the liberal interventionism of the 1990s: could the United States lead the developed world in times of relative peace to rebuild a major state along liberal principles, and would the world back that endeavor? Very quickly in Europe, and increasingly in the United States as the difficulties of state-building following the invasion became clear, liberals denied that the Iraq War was an appropriate test for their ideas.

Why should that be? Why would liberals who were happy to advocate intervention and state-building on a smaller scale and under similar legal circumstances shy away from backing regime change in Iraq? A number of reasons suggest themselves, but none of them amount to a rebuttal of the idea that the Iraq War sits firmly in the continuum of liberal policies.

The first potential explanation lies in the domestic political context of the Iraq experience, in which the case for the war lay firmly in United States' experience of September 11th. Unusually in post-Cold War interventions, it was not an operation that the world lobbied the United States to undertake, but one which the United States decided was required itself. Given that the United States had already launched a post-9/11 invasion in Afghanistan — in which it had largely rejected others' assistance — there was a perception that the liberal superpower was assuming a dangerous amount of responsibility for the liberal project. Allied to this were the suspicions about the motivations for the war, and particularly the idea that this was a war of imperial conquest for resources. Unilateralism, rather than the cause to which it was put, was the source of dissatisfaction that could be seen in liberal capitals around the world in early 2003.

The second reason for liberals to reject the liberal character of the Iraq War was that the Iraq War very swiftly came to be viewed as a failure that exposed the flaws in the liberal project. Beatte Jahn has shown convincingly that past failures of liberal state-building have rarely been accepted for what they are — that is, failures of the logic of the transition paradigm which sees development as a self-perpetuating process travelling smoothly in the direction of market democracy ("The Tragedy of Liberal Diplomacy," *Journal of Intervention and Statebuilding* 1, no. 1 and no. 2, 2007). Instead, failures are seen as failures of specific policies or are blamed on the lack of additional complementary policies. Thus, liberals add reform of state capacity and governance to the need for elections, and then add on top addressing weaknesses of indigenous culture, and so on and so on. It is this that leads to the necessity of what is essentially a deep, overarching and imperial policy to establish liberal market democracy. In Iraq, even that overarching liberal imperialism was exposed as a failure, and so the capacity of liberal ideology to reassert itself becomes dependent on the disavowal that Iraq was in fact a liberal war.

The final and certainly underestimated factor was that this was George W. Bush's war. Bush, a President who had stolen the Presidential election in 2000, an anti-abortion, pro-gun President who pandered to the religious right, a President who had responded to 9/11 with the Patriot Act, a President whose rejection of multilateral institutions had European liberals up in arms, a President who liberals considered, frankly, ignorant of the world at large and intellectually incapable. In the wider world as well as in America, Bush was a polarizing figure, his policies inspiring automatic opposition by the sheer fact of the person who had made them. In part, the anti-Americanism reflected in the Iraq protests was anti-Bush, and the world found in the person of George W. Bush an outlet for more general dissatisfaction with American foreign policy, a dissatisfaction that stemmed from American power on the one hand — and the triumphalism and cultural infiltration associated with it — and on the other hand, ironically, from America's refusal to use that power for *more* liberal ends, for example in Rwanda.

None of these potential explanations do liberals much credit. It says a great deal about how dominant the liberal orthodoxy had become, and how strong its lens for viewing international politics was, that many on the left of the political spectrum failed to understand both the logic of their own thinking and what it could be used to justify. At the heart of the issue is the tension inherent in the claim to universality of a doctrine of freedom of choice. If liberalism is universal, if the property in our own person is indeed innately ours, then one cannot willingly surrender that right, and the existence of illiberal forms of government necessarily evidences injustice. Free elections that produce illiberal outcomes must by definition be flawed. States who act to undermine the established liberal democracies cannot represent the will of their people.

Yet the prescriptions in defense of those oppressed peoples, from tied aid to intervention and state-building, themselves violate those liberal principles of free choice. The great liberal paradox is between letting people choose their own government — to the extent that they are able — and accepting the associate possibility that they may not choose a liberal form of government; and intervening to impose that form of government and violating those liberal principles of free choice in the first place.

It seems odd, counter-intuitive even, to suggest that enabling people to freely choose can be considered an imposition, and somewhat unsurprisingly it is within this apparent contradiction that the deep logical failure of the liberal interventionist project lies. The crucial flaw in liberal interventionism lies in the notion of intervention, in the idea that political liberty handed down in the form of democratic institutions and a market democracy can have the same character as home-grown liberalism. Or to put it another way, the interventionist project relies on the mistaken belief that the innate liberty of people that generates liberal politics can itself be satisfied by the creation of liberal political institutions. Human beings react not in gratitude for the availability of structures that enable their innate freedom, but in anger that their potential to create those structures for themselves has been usurped. An empire of liberty retains the character of empire, no matter how pure, benevolent and liberal its motives.

## Conclusion — Liberal Overstretch

In its liberal origins, the Iraq War represents a capitulation to the tyranny of orthodoxy, a mass derogation of the responsibility to question the dominant mode of thinking. Here was a liberal war, underscored by liberal assumptions, and waged in pursuit of liberal values. It was a war of liberal hubris, of overconfidence in the universal desirability of liberal values, but moreover in the failure to understand that having the right motives does not necessarily mean doing the right thing. In ideology too, power corrupts, and absolute power corrupts absolutely.

This ideological scaffolding of universal liberalism has long been a necessary precondition of a global, indeed even an international, role for the United States. During the Cold War, that scaffold legitimated an enduring commitment to the national interest conceived in terms of power and liberty, but in the post-Cold War world the material aspect of that national interest fell away and with it the constraints of a balance of power, leaving only an empire of ideology to make global the liberal peace. The lack of ideological alternatives rendered by this moment at the "end of history" left the United States — in its dominance of both ideas and power — as a kind of international socio-political *fait accompli* rather than a genuine expression of agreement. Large swathes of the world were left disappointed that their alignments and alliances in 40 years of proxy conflicts had bought them not stakes in the new world order but its interference.

Thus, that the Iraq War was possible is a story not just about the power of ideas but about the alliance of ideas with power — something that classical realists, including the great father of the American discipline Hans J. Morgenthau, had warned against. Entrusting an empire with world-making ideas is unlikely to be a satisfying exercise, and an overwhelming preponderance of power is liable to create illusions of the practicality of world-making. The tragedy of the Iraq War is that its liberal overstretch undermines the legitimacy of limited liberalism, of those ideas that provide the national interest with a particular ethic, a moral compass that helps constitute political identity. By doing too much too soon, in attempting to forcibly extend the liberal peace to Iraq, the United States has put at risk the steady drip of the liberalizing progress of history.

Of course, according to those who now proclaim the success of the surge and cite Iraq's progress in embedding and sustaining democratic norms, the problem of Iraq lay in practice, not theory. The lessons of Iraq are therefore lessons of too rapid a military victory, of stretched supply lines, of disbanding established social structures like the army rather than reforming them, of failing to recognize that democracy is not a panacea but has to go hand-in-hand with economic and political development. In this view Iraq's failure was one of details, of the tactics and policies employed on this specific occasion, rather than representing overriding flaws of liberal strategy and ideology.

The list of those initial failures of execution is long, starting with a lack of coherent post-war planning as highlighted by the bureaucratic musical chairs played by the Departments of Defense and State; Donald Rumsfeld's insistence on minimal troop numbers and a military "dash to Baghdad" that stretched supply lines and failed to pacify the country; the premature disbanding of the Iraqi army and the "de-Ba'thification" of the civil service; the reliance on private contractors for processes of reconstruction; Paul Bremer. All have been cited as precipitate causes of the failure to establish governance once military victory had been won and the Iraqi regime decapitated.

This view has become the received wisdom, overwhelmingly prominent among policymakers and also among scholars, and histories of the Iraq conflict are already beginning to reflect its maxims. While it may see Iraq as a war of choice, it believes its legacy must lie in learning lessons of implementation, not in considering the logic of the choice, and so it fails to adequately question the ideological origins of the war and their essential link to its catastrophic failure. Indeed, the supposed policy failures throw a mirror on the weaknesses of broader liberal assumptions about the transformative capacities of democratic institutions. The military approach to the war and the lack of concurrent commitment to building state capability reflect an underlying faith in liberalism that almost defies belief: it is as if policymakers believed that the blessings of liberty would magically produce social stability, prosperity and political consensus overnight.

The dominance of this viewpoint means that the apparent paradox of massive resistance to professed universal values is glossed over or ignored, and the logical inconsistencies in the liberal interventionist project that spawned Iraq are left uninterrogated. At the very least, when the values that we profess to be universal are apparently rejected, we should engage in a process of ideological soul-searching. Instead, the post-Iraq response from liberals has been to look for technical deficiencies, almost as if the task at hand is to learn how to "do it better next time." There is, of course, little desire in Washington or anywhere else for the "next time" to be anytime soon. But the danger, perhaps not now but certainly in years to come, when the memories have faded and the history has been written, is that in failing to recognize the liberal character of the Iraq War, liberals are condemned to repeat it.

Chapter 4

# The Crisis in Global Governance After the Iraq War

David Armstrong

## Introduction

Less than 20 years ago, the end of the Cold War and the success of the first Gulf War in 1991 had prompted a number of leading Americans to pronounce the beginning of a new global order. Led by President George Bush (senior), these statements spelt out a strategic vision with five key components, all of which were echoed by Bill Clinton during the 1992 election campaign.

First, the end of the Cold War was seen as a triumph of Western values such as democracy, human rights and the market economy. Second, American leadership was seen as both inevitable and desirable. "America must lead the world we have done so much to make", as Mr. Clinton put it, a sentiment echoed by Mr. Bush on numerous occasions. Third, the end of Soviet–American rivalry was seen as having freed the UN to perform the task originally envisaged for it, with the first Gulf War arriving opportunely to make the same point. Fourth, initial American assessments of the security situation in 1990–1991 envisaged a more peaceful world, with arms reductions, peace dividends and new concepts of "cooperative security" replacing the balance of terror. Close cooperation within NATO would help to establish this more secure world. Finally, there was to be an important economic dimension to the new global order, with the Group of Seven coordinating a shift by the emerging economies of Eastern

Europe and elsewhere towards market economies at the same time that the GATT promoted a more liberal trading order.

Clearly encouraged by the new atmosphere, UN Secretary-General Boutros Boutros-Ghali produced his 1992 report to the Security Council, *An Agenda for Peace*. In it, after proclaiming the opportunity that had arisen with the end of the Cold War to achieve the original objectives of the UN, he set out an ambitious program that in reality went well beyond the UN's original security mandate in an attempt to confront the much more complex challenges of the 1990s. These included "preventive diplomacy" to identify and work to prevent conflicts before they actually occurred, "peace-making" to bring hostile parties to peaceful settlement of their disputes, "peace-keeping" through UN forces to implement and maintain peace settlements, and "post-conflict peace-building" to help to lay down the bases for maintaining peace in the longer term. These were defined as "good governance", specifically, economic and social development together with the establishment of human rights regimes, the rule of law and democratic institutions. Although Boutros-Ghali did not spell this out in his report, what he envisaged would clearly involve intervention for humanitarian and other purposes in *internal* conflicts rather than in interstate disputes for which the UN was originally designed.

Notwithstanding numerous peacekeeping disappointments in the years following *An Agenda for Peace*, this essential theme of humanitarian intervention was still much in evidence in British Prime Minister Tony Blair's April 1999 Chicago speech, when he explicitly set out the case for the central UN Charter principle of non-intervention in the internal affairs of states to be qualified when the humanitarian case for intervention was unmistakeable.

Actual developments in international institutions and the international law they were upholding did, to some extent, reflect the underlying optimism about the role of such organizations in the new global order. Increasing concerns about environmental issues led to an extensive series of measures to combat ozone layer depletion following the Montreal Protocol of 1987 and later, the 1992 Rio Framework Convention on Climate Change and the 1997 Kyoto

Protocol setting out specific targets for states. Developments in the global economy included extensive changes, such as compulsory dispute settlement mechanisms, that led to the General Agreement on Tariffs and Trade (GATT) being transformed in 1995 into the World Trade Organization (WTO), the establishment of the European Central Bank in 1998, the introduction of the Euro from 1999–2002, and the expansion of IMF membership and of the use of structural adjustment programs and other forms of conditionality attached to loan agreements. The IMF, World Bank and UN were invited to the major powers' Group of Seven (G7) meetings in 1996. In other regions, the North American Free Trade Area (NAFTA) was established in 1994, while the Association of Southeast Asian Nations (ASEAN) expanded to include Indochina countries, with further measures of integration and liaison with China agreed after the Asian financial crisis of 1997. The New Partnership for African Development (NEPAD) was proposed in the late 1990s and eventually agreed upon in 2001.

Similarly in the security field, after the impetus given by the first Gulf War — arguably the UN's first true collective security operation — there was a huge expansion of UN involvement in security issues (15 Security Council resolutions were passed in 1987, 53 in 1991 and 78 in 1993). The UN was involved in 11 conflicts in 1987, 13 in 1991 and 28 in 1993, with its security budget expanding from $230 million in 1987 to $1,689 million in 1991 and $3,610 million in 1993. In line with the greater emphasis on intervention in humanitarian crises and punishment of those instigating them, the International Criminal Tribunal for Yugoslavia was established in 1993, the Rwandan equivalent in 1994, while the more far-reaching Rome Statute of the International Criminal Court was agreed in 1998. Other notable developments include the Ottawa Landmines Treaty of 1997, the signing by the EU of the Amsterdam Treaty of 1997 which included provisions for a common foreign and security policy, NATO's first ever direct military engagements in 1994–1999 in Yugoslavia, the 1998 UN Convention for the Suppression of Terrorist Bombings and the 1999 Convention for the Suppression of the Financing of Terrorism.

It is, perhaps, ironic to recall some of the debate provoked by the American rhetoric about a new global order and the more interventionist policies during the 1990s to which it gave rise. Conservative Americans revived apprehensions about the implications for US sovereignty and threats to the American Constitution from what they saw as relinquishing power to international organizations. These were similar apprehensions to those that had surfaced on occasion in US politics ever since the Senate was unable to pass the Versailles Treaty in 1919, with the consequence that the US did not enter the newly formed League of Nations. The Clinton administration came under particular attack for its so-called "surrender" of American power to the UN and other organizations. Indeed, it was criticism of this kind that led in 1994 to Clinton's Presidential Decision Directive 25 (PDD 25), under which the US was to reduce its financial commitment to UN peacekeeping and limit its actual involvement in peacekeeping to missions under American command and that served America's national interests. PDD 25 was invoked in 1994 to prevent a stronger UN response to the genocide in Rwanda. Those of a more left-liberal persuasion developed variants of a "New American Empire" thesis alongside arguments about the potential and actual damage to fragile economies arising from the imposition of structural adjustment policies. Some went so far as to maintain that IMF structural adjustment policies in Yugoslavia during the 1980s had done much to create the increasing insecurity and falling economic growth that created the conditions which eventually led to the genocidal horrors of the 1990s. A few years later, the former Chief Economist at the World Bank, Joseph Stiglitz, was likewise to blame similar IMF policies for the Asian economic crisis of 1997. The anti-globalization movement listed both the IMF and the WTO amongst its leading targets — again implicitly working from a perception of those organizations as very powerful international actors. Others focused on what they saw as the dangers of the new interventionism. For example, some argued that the humanitarian intervention norm might, paradoxically, encourage genocidal violence because rebel groups might feel incentivized to continue their struggles in the hope of provoking a brutal response that might lead to international intervention. What all these criticisms had in common was a perception that a new global order was indeed emerging, with an enhanced role for international institutions at its heart.

Writing in 2009, a rather different narrative amounting to nothing less than a major crisis for multilateralism and global governance can easily be constructed. George W. Bush's Presidency, even before 9/11, had trumpeted an emphatically unilateralist doctrine that, in the course of his Presidency, gave rise to numerous specific policy decisions that had the effect of weakening the global governance foundations for the new world order that his father had declared in 1993. These included ignoring the necessity for Security Council approval for major uses of force in the Iraq War, refusing to accept the Kyoto Protocol on climate change and the Ottawa Convention on landmines, weakening the nuclear non-proliferation regime in various ways even while invoking it against Iran and North Korea, withdrawing from the Anti-Ballistic Missile Treaty, and rejecting and working against the Rome Treaty establishing the International Criminal Court. Perhaps its most symbolic expression of contempt for multilateralism was its appointment of the hardline and combative neo-conservative, John Bolton, as US Ambassador to the United Nations in 2005.

The crisis of multilateralism and international governance went well beyond the Bush Presidency, although the somewhat buccaneering approach of his administration after 9/11 was certainly a major contributor to the more widespread climate of narrow pursuit of self-interest and disregard for global governance that was increasingly evident. For example, the failure of the Doha Round of trade talks in July 2008 was seen by many as potentially damaging to the WTO. The IMF was virtually invisible as the 2008 global financial crisis unfolded. Even the most successful international organization, the European Union, found itself unable to secure popular approval first for its proposed Constitution, then for the watered-down version of this, the Lisbon Treaty. A resurgent Russia contemptuously ignored UN rules concerning the legitimate use of force during its 2008 intervention in Georgia, arguing that the United States and NATO had behaved similarly over the Kosovo crisis. In October 2008 two

ASEAN members, Thailand and Cambodia, exchanged fire over a disputed territory, while Indonesia planned a naval exercise with the aim of confronting another fellow-member, Malaysia, over disputed waters. This was in the same month that the ASEAN Charter — with its ambitious provisions for strengthening cooperation in security, economic and human rights areas — was ratified. Meanwhile, in Africa, NEPAD, the other African organizations and the UN were all relatively powerless in the face of continuing conflict in the Congo, Sudan and elsewhere as well as the collapse of Zimbabwe and other crises.

In the remainder of this chapter, I shall examine in more detail the argument that we are facing a crisis of global governance of major proportions and consider possible ways forward. But first, some of the key terms I shall be using need to be more carefully defined.

## The Nature of Global Governance

The starting point for much academic discussion of international relations is the fact that, because states are seen as legally sovereign entities, they neither acknowledge any superior authority nor can they rely on any external force for their security other than themselves. They are, therefore, doomed to exist in a state of permanent competition and struggle for power: an international anarchy. In reality, this bleak, Hobbesian picture of war of all against all has seldom, if ever, provided an accurate portrayal of what actually goes on between states and, in the period since 1945, international relations have increasingly been subject to an ever-more complex structure of rules, institutions, mechanisms and procedures that may most appropriately be termed a structure of global governance.

While the term "government" may be defined as authority exercised over a given community backed by extensive powers of revenue generation and enforcement, "governance" is a much looser, more complex term. Broadly speaking, it denotes *rules, structures* and *processes* providing some measure of regulation over specific areas of activity and working towards certain given objectives. Such rules, structures and processes may be *formal* or *informal*. Governance tends to work through less coercive enforcement powers than government — one reason why it is an appropriate term for international affairs — and with substantially less capacity to generate revenue. In global politics, the term is used in three contexts, although the distinctions between these are not always precise and the reality is frequently that actual governance may take place with elements of all three:

- *International Governance.* This is where the actors are mainly states and the objectives relate mainly to the regulation of *interstate* relations. For example, the United Nations is an interstate organization designed — at least in its initial conception — to deal with tensions over security and other issues arising between governments.
- *Global Governance.* This involves states and intergovernmental organizations as well as transnational and national non-state actors. Its objectives are more complex and wide-ranging than those of international governance, mainly because it is concerned with the regulation of broad areas of interaction involving this wide range of actors. For example, global economic affairs are subject to the rules of intergovernmental organizations such as the WTO, the World Bank and the IMF, as well as national and regional regulations applying to transnational corporations, with a constant input from non-governmental organizations and other non-state actors from what we may term global civil society. Numerous private authorities constitute a large, complex global network that creates and implements regulatory regimes in a wide range of areas, including insurance, credit ratings, labor standards, aspects of the environment and the Internet. Transnational social movements also make various kinds of inputs to these regimes. In some cases such as the war in Iraq, a small group of states such as the US and its "coalition of the willing" may claim to be acting in the interests of global governance; in other cases, this may be a responsibility undertaken by a regional or global institution. As the broadest of the three usages of the term "governance" in world affairs, "global governance" may also be employed, as it is in this paper, as a shorthand expression for all three types of governance.

- *Regional Governance.* This may be seen as a subset of global governance applicable to a specific region. By far the most developed example here is the European Union, where powerful institutional actors such as the Commission, the Council, the European Parliament and the Court of Justice apply the ever increasing array of EU regulations in a context of constant political and lobbying activities from a range of national and regional actors, including national governments and parliaments, political parties, trade unions and NGOs.

Governance of any kind tends to be assessed by virtue of its *effectiveness* and *legitimacy*. Both involve more complex considerations than government (where legitimacy may be seen as a product of elections or other measures of popular approval, and effectiveness as a product of successful use of the wide powers available to government). In the international/global context, *effectiveness* may perhaps be defined as the capacity to achieve set objectives without undue disruption and *legitimacy* in terms of a broad degree of acceptance by those affected by governance. The crisis in global governance that has been outlined here in the crucial issue areas of security, the environment and economics/finance is, in part, a crisis of both legitimacy and effectiveness, and it is to this that I now turn. I shall consider primarily, although not exclusively, the security area, since this is the one that relates most closely to the question of global order in the aftermath of the Iraq War.

## The Crisis in Global Governance

Understandings of the nature of security in the contemporary era have evolved considerably since the days when the primary focus was on the military (especially nuclear) balance between the two superpowers. Today, most analysts favor a much broader understanding of the term, so that, for example, economic and social causes of conflict within states and concepts like "human security" have become part of both academic discourse on security and policy frameworks of specific peace missions. Within that broad context, five distinct types of security questions are currently high on the international agenda, and each of them poses its own set of global governance issues. First, the global balance of power between the major states is gradually changing with the rise of China and India and the revival of Russian power. Each of these states has its own security concerns and objectives, and each of these in turn has the potential to produce major new global tensions. China, for example, has unresolved territorial disputes with several of its neighbors including Japan, and it also has a longstanding aspiration to incorporate Taiwan, a country currently enjoying US protection. India's conflict with Pakistan over Kashmir and other issues has already come close to war in the new century, with fresh tensions being aroused in the aftermath of the Mumbai terrorist attacks in November 2008. Meanwhile, Putin's Russia is determined to reassert its interests in its former Soviet neighboring states at the same time that they have been seeking NATO membership.

Secondly, there is the range of security issues that may be loosely grouped together under the heading of "terrorism". These should be treated with particular care by any analyst since, in reality, they derive from many quite distinct problems and are far from being a single phenomenon, and also because dramatic media coverage has sometimes given them a prominence they do not always warrant. Nonetheless, perceptions create their own reality and some variant of a "war on terror" is high on the security agenda of most major states. Groups employing terror tactics such as suicide attacks do so in the interest of highlighting a particular set of issues and also, frequently, of provoking a harsh response that might help them to win new recruits. A particular set of apprehensions revolve around the possibility of a terrorist group employing weapons of mass destruction.

Thirdly, the post-Cold War phenomenon of collapsing and fragmenting states has given rise to many security issues, mainly in Africa. These include the danger of a conflict in one country spilling over into others, especially when neighboring countries compete for influence in a collapsed state, and the range of security questions arising from the increasing tendency to grant various kinds of international legal rights (and therefore corresponding international duties to protect) to individuals. It was these cases that Boutros-Ghali's aforementioned *An Agenda for Peace* was particularly designed to address. More recently, the success of pirates operating from the collapsed state of Somalia in the Gulf of Aden and Indian Ocean has raised major issues relating to the security of important shipping routes.

Fourthly, there is an increasing danger of nuclear proliferation and a correspondingly higher risk of nuclear weapons being employed in interstate conflict now than at any other time in the last 30 years. This has been a constant threat in Indo–Pakistan relations, and also arises in the context of the acquisition of such weapons by unpredictable regimes in North Korea and (potentially) Iran. In the latter case, there is also the possibility of a preemptive attack by Israel or the United States.

Finally, the Middle East more generally remains a cauldron of various tensions, including those surrounding Iraq, the Palestine issue, Lebanon, Iranian hegemonial aspirations, the Sunni–Sh'ia divide, and the complex politics of oil and water.

Four central questions of global governance arise from these security concerns, the first of which revolves around issues relating to *legitimacy*. The UN Charter stipulates that force may only be used legitimately in self-defence in the face of an immediate threat or with the approval of a majority of the Security Council, including all five permanent members (the P5). This was a major issue in the American-led invasion of Iraq, which some saw as opening the doors to a more general readiness by major powers to ignore the UN. Wider issues of legitimate global governance have been raised in regards to the Security Council itself, with critics focusing on the veto powers of the P5 and the fact that the current permanent membership was decided more than 60 years ago and does not reflect the many changes since then. Similar issues have been raised about the voting power of the major Western states and Japan in the IMF and World Bank.

A different kind of legitimacy question revolves around the frequent misconduct of UN peacekeeping troops, given that UN interventions are obviously assumed to employ higher moral standards than the warring parties they seek to separate. Accusations have ranged from murder to child rape and torture. The same kinds of issues arose in the context of American and British mistreatment of prisoners during the Iraq War and the American use of its Guantanamo Bay facilities to evade the legal issues relating to the rights of the prisoners that would have been unavoidable if they had been taken to the US. Another related issue derives from the fact that an intervention may — intentionally or unintentionally — aid one side in an internal conflict, thus causing the enemies of that side to reject the legitimacy of an intervention.

Such misconduct, combined with the perception of many in Iraq and Afghanistan that their lives might actually have been better under Saddam or the Taliban, has raised a final legitimacy issue: the "good governance" (democracy, human rights and public accountability) that Western-led intervention forces have tried to impose has increasingly been depicted as an attempt to impose an agenda of Western values that is inappropriate to the target states. "Global governance", in other words, is merely disguised Western neo-imperialism by this argument.

The second set of general issues relating to governance concerns *effectiveness*. Complex political problems can seldom, if ever, be resolved purely by the application of force, which may in fact make matters much worse. This has arguably been the case in Iraq, where, even before the war, the UN sanctions regime was already contributing to thousands of deaths and, when fighting started, the US initially seemed to be operating on the assumption that its mission would be accomplished once the regime of Saddam Hussein was overthrown. Such consequences of the war as increased anti-Western sentiments amongst some sections of the global Muslim community, large-scale internal conflict in Iraq itself, and intervention by external forces ranging from Iran to al-Qaeda, do not appear to have been seriously contemplated by the American decision makers, even though all were predicted by many regional experts at the time.

Different kinds of effectiveness issues have been raised in connection with UN operations, where inefficiencies, corruption and inter-agency squabbling have not helped the UN to perform its mandate in several conflict zones, especially given the severe cost restraints under which it often operates. Perhaps the most common effectiveness problem in multilateral actions is the difficulty of ensuring coordinated and efficient command and control of operational forces where the troops concerned work from different manuals and levels of training and with varying political constraints from their ultimate masters, namely their own national governments. This was seen even in the Afghanistan conflict where, although the mainly NATO forces did by and large operate with shared combat understandings, training, etc., different levels of national governmental enthusiasm for the war led to more than 70 national "caveats" restricting the military roles of about 40 participating states.

Thirdly, there are fundamental issues relating to *agency*. If the implementation of national government is carried out by clearly demarcated agents such as police forces and courts of law and enforced by punishments including fines and imprisonment, who acts on behalf of global governance? Even when the international community has been able to reach agreement on the necessity for a particular operation, the overwhelming preponderance of American military power and its higher levels of technological sophistication mean, in practice, that any complex operation will require a substantial American contribution. This was most clearly seen in the various NATO and UN interventions in former Yugoslavia during the 1990s, where even the relatively sophisticated military forces of the leading European states did not possess the advanced air power that was needed in operations like the Kosovo intervention. At another level, however, effective peace-building often requires a major input from non-governmental organizations (NGOs). Hence, in one case "global governance" may involve an essentially American agency, whereas in another "governance" emanates from non-state elements. In either case, additional issues of fairness or equity are also raised since the United States will generally only apply its military power where it perceives American interests to be involved, while NGOs tend to have their own particular interests and are of course limited in terms of the resources at their disposal.

Finally, there is the complex range of questions stemming from the never-ending conflict between the demand for two kinds of values in international relations: *order* and *justice*. At the risk of oversimplification, the tasks of national governments may be defined as balancing the demands of citizens for these two values. The first involves objectives such as regularity, predictability and stability in the operations of the state's legal, security and political organs so that individuals can lead their lives with some assurance as to their personal safety and of the continuity of the institutions of the society to which they belong. Justice is notoriously more difficult to define with any degree of precision, but in political discourse it is generally taken to have two main components: *procedural justice*, so that the processes through which various kinds of decisions are taken by organs of power such as parliaments and courts are generally accepted as functioning reasonably fairly; and *distributive justice*, which means that all should be able to share to some extent in a society's wealth — for example, by receiving a free education or financial support when unemployed or disabled.

In global politics, demands are likewise frequently heard for both order and justice, and debate about global justice tends to follow similar paths to the domestic equivalent. The desire for decisions to be perceived as legitimate, for example, is in part an aspect of procedural justice, while pressure for more aid to poor countries reflects a desire for distributive justice. However, the pursuit of both order and justice in global society has clearly encountered far greater obstacles than those experienced in most states — certainly in the more prosperous states. The main explanation for this is to be found in the differences between government and governance as outlined here, with the latter lacking the extensive coercive and revenue generative powers of the former. A related explanation concerns the fact that individuals tend to identify far more closely with the national society to which they belong and pay taxes than with the larger global community. For example, it is impossible to imagine an American government surviving very long if it stood by while the people of Oregon or Texas had a life expectancy that was half that of the people of New York or if more than 10% of the population of California had been killed or raped during widespread violence, as has happened in many parts of Africa.

A similar problem concerns the nature of the community to which principles of justice should apply. For example, international law embodies notions of justice that derive from an underlying conception of a society of sovereign states. In this, *procedural* justice consists of ensuring that each state has equal rights in certain decision making fora, such as the General Assembly of the United Nations. However, as we shall see below, justice conceived as securing equal rights of all to fulfilment of basic needs such as food entails a different conception of the society within which justice is pursued: the cosmopolitan idea of a global community of human beings. There is clearly considerable scope at the very least for the collision of these two societal frameworks, if not for their ultimate irreconcilability.

## Ways Forward?

I have suggested here that the three great global crises of our time — in security, economics and finance, and the environment — have each been accompanied (and in part caused) by a parallel crisis in global governance. Although proposals for improving the ways in which the world is ordered have been heard from time to time for hundreds of years, the last 10 years have witnessed an intense debate in international institutions and in numerous non-governmental and academic circles about the best way forward for global governance. The following represents, in broad outline, the main proposals that have emerged from this discourse.

### *Cosmopolitanism*

The starting point here is that we live in a global community of people, not simply an international society of states, and global governance should reflect that rather than merely act to minimize interstate conflict. When confronted by arguments that such propositions are little more than fanciful idealism, advocates of cosmopolitanism tend to argue that the complex range of processes collectively termed "globalization" has made the world increasingly interdependent, and this in turn has made a global community not just an abstract ideal but an everyday reality. This is most obviously true in the case of the environment, where the various dangers clearly do not observe national territorial boundaries, but it is also true of global economic and financial dynamics and of health.

The globalization of security risks is a more complex matter since the immediate victims of any conflict are obviously the people living in the affected area. But internal or interstate violence may have many indirect consequences such as refugees, easier availability of weapons that might fall into the hands of terrorists, and the possibility of lawlessness in collapsed states spilling over into other states and recently into piracy. All these demonstrate the near-impossibility of even an internal war remaining within the borders of the affected state.

The Internet and advances in electronic communication more generally have also created a global community of another kind. Here, events and developments can have an instantaneous impact — something that has been exploited by many international actors from terrorists to derivatives traders in financial markets and to famine relief NGOs.

What the cosmopolitanists argue is that globalization has already produced not just a global community but an emergent global governance which can be built upon. In support of this claim, they point to the increasing number of international regimes in areas like human rights, child labor, the environment and women's rights, together with the use of cosmopolitan terms like "the common heritage of mankind" to refer to outer space or the mineral resources of the seabed. However, the central problem with the cosmopolitan approach to governance is that, while it is relatively easy to sketch out its central principles, it is hard to work out how precisely to enshrine them in actual mechanisms of global governance. For example, cosmopolitanists believe that the use of reason within global communication processes to which all have equal access will lead to policy outcomes acceptable to all and which meet the greatest human needs and confront the worst kinds of harm. Such communication would take place within a common framework of assumptions about human rights in a world in which individuals are conceived as free and equal. Hence, governance would consist of a structure of institutional arrangements guided by, and owing primary allegiance to, this universal set of moral principles and which would not be dominated by the most powerful.

The two most fundamental difficulties with this vision are, first, whether there are indeed universal moral principles in a world containing completely opposite but equally strongly held views about the rights of women or gays or about issues such as capital punishment and freedom of speech. Secondly, such a new global order could only come about following a surrender by the most powerful states of their global power. Even in the unlikely event of such a transformation, it is hard to imagine precisely what form the "institutional arrangements" that are suggested by the cosmopolitanists might take. For example, any global democratic decision making process would, presumably, be based primarily on some form of majority voting. The Chinese population is currently greater than the combined populations of North America, Europe and Japan, and unless the peoples of the latter three regions could be convinced that the Chinese people would consistently vote as global rather than Chinese citizens, it is unlikely that they would yield any meaningful democratic control over their own lives to such a "global community."

In response to such objections, cosmopolitanists might point to the success of the European Union in bringing about in one region something fairly close to the cosmopolitan dream for the whole world, with powerful member states accepting constraints on their own absolute sovereignty, individuals enjoying human rights enforceable at the European level and poorer regions receiving aid based on need. However, while the EU has unquestionably confounded many sceptical pronouncements as well as overcoming strong resistance from nationalist leaders like France's De Gaulle and Britain's Thatcher, Europe is a special case in many respects with, by and large, a common culture and also a history of catastrophic 20th century wars and human rights violations on a massive scale that convinced enough of its leaders that serious alternative approaches were required. Even then, since enlargement, there is a great deal of evidence that European peoples — when they have been given the choice — will resist further deepening of the Union.

## Multilateralism and the rule of law

A less idealistic and ambitious perspective on global governance than that offered by cosmopolitanism starts from the premise that the main problems with the contemporary international system revolve around the legitimacy crisis discussed above. Like cosmopolitanists, proponents of this position identify the most powerful states as a major part of this problem but, unlike them, they do not call for a shift from a society of states to a community of individuals. Instead, they argue for more limited reforms that would embody the two central principles of multilateralism and the rule of law. The first of these expresses the belief that international decision making that is clearly seen to have taken place within a context that enables genuine contributions from significant numbers of states is more legitimate than one that simply reflects the dominance of a few powerful states. The specific nature of the context may be formal or informal, so long as it is founded upon generally accepted understandings about essential norms and rules of conduct.

Multilateralism does not necessarily exclude a hegemonial role by a single power: in the 19th century Britain played such a role with respect to the financial and trading order, while the post-war order was largely constructed and underwritten by the United States. This is where the second principle of the rule of law becomes crucial because it encapsulates the notion that all are equally bound by the obligations involved in any multilateral regime. Multilateralism is a term that is mainly used today to refer to the interactions among sovereign states acting collectively. The rule of law concept is more complex. In essence, it refers to a specific set of requirements which evolved to put into practice the idea that the only way to protect individuals from the arbitrary exercise of power is to subject all within the state to the ultimate authority of the law. The logical extension of this argument is the view that the legal system in its entirety needs to exist as an autonomous sphere of action, utilizing a professional class of highly trained jurists able to base their deliberations purely on legal considerations rather than on moral, political, ideological or other factors. Laws should, furthermore, be clear, not retrospective, general and consistent in their application, give rise to stable and predictable expectations, and be interpreted and administered through well-established and widely understood procedures.

It is immediately apparent that implementing this fully in the global sphere raises some of the same kinds of problems already encountered in the discussion of cosmopolitanism. On the one hand, many have argued strongly that the American-led Iraq War lacked legitimacy essentially because it flouted the principle of the international rule of law. On the other hand, the United States, which possesses military power equal to the next nine major states, is highly unlikely to reduce its power in order to conform with a principle of the international rule of law that is nowhere near as well-entrenched as it is, for example, in the United States itself. Nor is it necessarily the case that such a fully-fledged legal structure is entirely appropriate to the international sphere. Indeed — at least in its most adversarial Anglo-Saxon mode — it could actually push states into confrontations where more traditional processes of resolving differences through diplomacy might be more effective.

This is not to argue that international law does not have an increasingly important place in sustaining global order through its role in establishing clear and agreed rules in many areas. Even the United States discovered value in seeking UN Security Council legitimation of its actions and wider UN involvement in peace-making activities within months of its intervention, to a point where the term "multilateralism" was probably heard more often from George W. Bush than from any other world leader. The new American President, Barack Obama, has also appealed to multilateralism and the international rule of law in both rhetoric and some actions. However, the international political reality is that major powers will accept more representative and accountable processes of international decision making as well as greater legalization of international affairs only while they perceive it to be in their interests to do so, and they will retain the ability to opt out of such multilateral arrangements. The rule of law within a state is backed up by effective sanctions against lawbreakers of a kind that do not exist in respect of the more powerful states.

## UN reform

The post-Cold War era has highlighted numerous shortcomings in the United Nations as the principal institution responsible for upholding global order, and the last 15 years in particular have witnessed a vast array of proposals from within and outside the UN for its reform. Apart from the issues concerning Security Council membership, which I have already touched upon, numerous managerial and bureaucratic issues have been identified, including the lack of coordination between UN agencies and of any real, coherent overall management of the agencies; the ability of the General Assembly to vote for an endless series of programs, reports and other initiatives whose purpose often seems little more than to employ numerous officials in pointless pen-pushing; and increasing disillusionment and cynicism amongst lower-level administrators (evidenced in an open letter in May 2008 to UN Secretary-General Ban Ki Moon complaining about nepotism and favoritism in senior staff appointments and relatively low levels of pay).

A great deal of criticism has focused on the inadequacies of the UN's Department of Peacekeeping Operations, although some of these are a consequence of the fact that it was staffed and oriented to carry out the fairly static peacekeeping operations that had been the norm during the Cold War. This problem was exacerbated by the fact that the financial crisis induced by the American refusal to pay their dues had the effect of freezing recruitment to the UN from 1985. In a 1995 article, former Secretary-General Perez de Cuellar identified four ways in which the UN had been inadequately prepared: (1) the UN had lacked adequate funding, managerial staff and command and control procedures for expanded peacekeeping operations; (2) it had no real guidelines or precedents for dealing with internal conflicts of the kind that now faced it; (3) it lacked appropriately trained troops in sufficient numbers and with the necessary equipment; and (4) it had no mechanism for coordinating and integrating the work of its functional agencies in humanitarian crises — in fact, the 1990s were marked by various unseemly turf wars between different UN agencies. Since then, many other proposals have been put forward to improve UN peacekeeping and in particular to separate its political from its operational aspects, but these have failed to make much progress.

Other criticisms have focused on the fact that UN bodies inevitably reflect political differences within the world they represent. For example, the UN's Commission on Human Rights failed to criticize many states responsible for serious human rights violations, such as Zimbabwe and Libya, whilst repeatedly attacking Israel — a pattern repeated in its successor organization, the Council for Human Rights. This reflected the alliance between the Arab world and other developing states that dominated the General Assembly. The same was true when, during his period as Secretary-General, Kofi Annan proposed that programs and other activities mandated by the General Assembly should be subject to five-year reviews of their continuing value, with the UN also having the capacity to shift resources from one program to another in accordance with need. This was blocked by the developing state alliance, the Group of 77. Conversely, the P5 in the Security Council have used their veto power to protect their own interests: the United States has consistently blocked resolutions attacking Israel, while China and Russia have done the same where their economic or strategic interests have been involved, most recently in the case of resolutions criticizing Zimbabwe and Myanmar. They have also resisted proposals to weaken their own power in the Security Council, although proposals to expand the permanent membership have generally failed to make headway due to regional rivalries regarding the various contenders — Pakistan is opposed to India's case, Argentina to Brazil's, Italy to Germany's, and Korea and China to Japan's. Nor would Security Council enlargement necessarily aid in resolving the problem of ineffectiveness without a huge additional commitment of resources by all members.

Many other specific proposals for reform have been advanced. For example, one suggestion is that, rather than working to change the UN, it might be better to sharply reduce what the UN actually does, to a point where it is little more than a place where major issues can be debated but implementation of security operations or humanitarian assistance would be delegated to regional organizations. The UN would remain the chief source of global legitimacy, but not much more.

There is in fact no end to proposals for UN reform, some of which focus on the General Assembly rather than the Council. The fact is that much of the increase in UN membership since the mid-1960s is accounted for by states with very small populations. 68 states have been admitted since 1966, making up 35% of General Assembly members, but these states only account for 9% of the world's population. Some states with populations of around 100,000 have the same vote as China with 1.5 billion people. In a similar vein, 15 countries pay 81% of the UN's budget, while 96 countries pay between them only 1.1%. This has led to calls for some sort of weighted voting system in the General Assembly, particularly from Western members who have been irritated by the Assembly's criticism of them. But again, proposals for reforming the Assembly run into the same problem that states will jealously guard their sovereignty. There are organizations — notably the European Union — which have weighted voting systems, but the smaller members here accept that because membership brings very concrete benefits.

The Economic and Social Council has long been a target of criticism. It is seen as unwieldy, with 54 states as members, 6 functional commissions, 5 regional commissions, 6 standing committees and 18 specialized agencies reporting to it, each engaged in empire building and turf wars and often duplicating each other's work. The 2005 World Summit made various proposals for reform, including creating a new body to coordinate development work. This came into being in 2008, but it is too early to tell whether it will make a substantive difference or simply add another layer of bureaucracy. There are also many proposals for getting the UN out of its financial difficulties, such as taxes on foreign exchange transactions, a UN stamp, a tax on air travel and the like. Here, too, we encounter a reality check. The cost of the UN to most governments is actually not very high, even for the United States. If governments are genuinely interested in improving the UN's capacity for action, it would not be too difficult for them, first to reduce the American share of contributions, and second to double or even treble the total UN budget. But if the major powers do not have the political will to do that, they are unlikely to accept measures that would at the same time make the UN more powerful as well as less dependent on them.

A similar point can be made of proposals to make the UN more "democratic" by engaging it more with global civil society — that is to say, with the enormous number of non-governmental organizations and social movements around the world. This, it is said, would put it more in touch with popular opinion and help to make it more transparent and accountable. NGOs already have the right of being registered as consultants to the ECOSOC, so this would, it is argued, simply extend that process. But there are two problems with proposals of this kind. First, most of these NGOs are self-appointed. There is no particular reason why they should be taken as representing anyone but themselves and the special interests they stand for. In other words, they themselves suffer from the same kind of "democratic deficit" they accuse the UN of having. Secondly, if the aim is to make the UN more effective, that would not necessarily be served by making it more democratic.

## Conclusion

There is, sadly, a high probability that some global problems will simply worsen. The essential politico-legal reality of the world will remain its division into sovereign states. Intervention into internal affairs will be very much the exception rather than the rule. Geopolitical realities will continue — probably for some decades — to give the United States a substantial margin of military power over other contenders, with fewer than 10 other states having any significant influence. Major developing states like China and India will inevitably add to the problem of global warming as their economies grow, even if the United States and Europe prove able to reduce their greenhouse gas emissions. The problem of collapsed and fragmented states will continue and possibly worsen. For the reasons that have been outlined here, it is unlikely that we will see any serious shift towards a cosmopolitan world order or even a more limited transformation in the current structure of global governance. But this does not necessarily mean a collapse into uncontrolled anarchy. Such global governance as we have today comprises a huge variety of mechanisms and processes, ranging from quite detailed and specific regimes in areas like trade to *ad hoc*, inconsistently applied and variable responses to security and humanitarian emergencies. These will continue to make such contributions as they do and may even evolve in more effective ways: it is possible, for example, that the global financial crisis might lead to a more regulated financial order. Moreover, although the United States has recently been criticized for its unilateralism, the reality is that it remains the leading provider of various global public goods and that much of the existing set of multilateral institutions was largely the creation of the United States, which saw them as a means of achieving some of its larger objectives through cooperation rather than conflict. If the more imaginative and less belligerent leadership promised by President Obama materializes, an American-led world order might be more widely acceptable.

Nor should we automatically see this limited, complex mixture of multilateralism and unilateralism, substantial regimes and *ad hoc* responses to events as a worse outcome than a much more formalized, comprehensive structure of global governance. The latter would also create its own set of massive problems and would not necessarily be more effective or democratic than what exists today. When Karl Popper, in *The Open Society and Its Enemies*, argued against absolutist approaches to knowledge in favor of Western pluralism, he also called for what he termed "piecemeal social engineering". By this, essentially, he meant acting not on the basis of some utopian vision, but as a result of trial and error and gradual improvement. Piecemeal international social engineering might be seen by some as little more than a call for "muddling through", given the dimensions of the problems we face today, but it might also be seen as an approach to global governance that both recognizes and builds upon the world's rich diversity.

## Chapter 5

# Terrorist Threat in Iraq: Origins, Development and Impact

### Rohan Gunaratna

### Introduction

An unpopular invasion, the US-led coalition occupation of Iraq, which began on 20 March 2003, dramatically transformed the global, regional and national threat landscape. No invasion in contemporary times, including the Soviet invasion of Afghanistan on Christmas Day in 1979, has had the profound national security impact as the invasion of Iraq. For Iraq, the invasion had multiple outcomes. The civil conflict produced human suffering, virulent ideologies, sectarian violence, internal displacement, refugee flows, and extremists and terrorists. The most enduring outcomes included: (a) the origin and development of national and regional threat groups, (b) the reorientation of groups to develop ideological and operational links with al-Qaeda, and (c) the relocation to Iraq of foreign threat groups, notably al-Qaeda. Today, these indigenous and foreign threat groups with terrorist and insurgent capabilities pose a threat to Iraq, the region and the world. Even after US disengagement, Iraq presents a suitable climate and a fertile environment for the continuing presence of a diverse range of threat groups. A fountain of poisonous ideology and lethal technology, these groups mount both domestic and international terrorist operations.

The Soviet invasion of Afghanistan (1979–1989) radicalized a generation of Muslim youth. Its repetition by the US in Iraq (2003–2009) has radicalized a wider segment of the Muslim community. Given that al-Qaeda, its associated groups and affiliated cells extensively use new media technologies (notably the Internet), the Iraq invasion has radicalized a generation. The proliferation of ideas, technology and tactics in Iraq in reality and in cyberspace will sustain the global terrorist and extremist threat in the foreseeable future. In terms of the sustained and uncontrolled violence in Iraq, the suffering of Iraqis and their Muslim brothers worldwide, the spawning and reinforcement of virulent ideologies, and the global impact, there is no comparable conflict. While the greater threat stems from within Iraq, its immediate neighborhood of the Levant will never be the same again. Securing the world, including future Iraq, from the fallout of the US invasion of Iraq will be a monumental challenge in the foreseeable future.

## The Context

The US-led coalition invasion of Iraq on 20 March 2003 created an uncertain global security climate, especially in the Muslim world. An unintended consequence of invasion was the emergence of Iraq as one of the most important global epicenters for insurgent, terrorist and extremist activity. Another consequence was the spillover effect of the insurgency and terrorist campaign into its immediate neighborhood, threatening and destabilizing countries around and in the vicinity of Iraq. Yet another enduring outcome was the politicization, radicalization and mobilization of a segment of Muslims worldwide, and of their local and regional threat groups. The US invasion of Iraq created an anti-Western Muslim transnational support base facilitating the transformation of al-Qaeda into a global movement. As the al-Qaeda family of groups seeks to identify its struggle as a *jihad*, it can be referred to as the global jihad movement.

Contrary to public opinion, al-Qaeda — the most hunted terrorist group in history led by Osama bin Laden — had established a presence in Iraq before the US invasion in 2003. A few threat groups located in the north of Iraq, notably the Islamic Movement of Kurdistan (IMK), had developed links with al-Qaeda in the 1990s. After the terrorist training and operational infrastructure in Afghanistan was dismantled by the US-led coalition intervention in Afghanistan in 2001, al-Qaeda and several other threat groups selected northern Iraq, a no-fly zone protected by the West, to establish a large-scale, enduring presence in Iraq. The Kurdish Islamists played a decisive role in planting the seeds and providing a platform for the launch of a campaign of insurgency. After the US invasion, the threat from the Kurdish areas of Iraq percolated to the middle of Iraq, and then to the rest of Iraq. From Iraq, the threat from Sunni groups spread to the region and beyond. As the Sunni groups were the best organized, many Baathists (especially former regime elements) and nationalists joined them. Both the Baathists and the nationalists organized and formed their own threat groups. The threat from Shia groups, including those sponsored by Iran, spread from the south to the center of Iraq. The IMK, the oldest threat group formed to fight Saddam Hussein, splintered into multiple groups. These groups included Kata'ib al Tawhid (Brigades of Faith), Komala Islami Kurdistan (Islamic Society of Kurdistan), and Ansar al Islam fi Kurdistan (Supporters of Islam in Kurdistan). The latter worked with foreign fighters including foreign threat groups such as Tawhid Wal Jihad (The Group for the Oneness of God and Jihad), which later renamed itself "al-Qaeda in Iraq."

The threat groups in Iraq can be divided into four classes: the Baathists (pro-Saddam Hussein), the Sunni nationalists, the Sunni Islamists (pro–al-Qaeda), and the Shia Islamists (pro-Iran). The Sunni insurgency is not a monolithic threat.[1] Iraq's most powerful Sunni insurgent group, the Islamic Army (Al-Jaish Al-Islamy), was founded in February 2004.[2] The al-Qaeda–led Islamic State of Iraq (Dawlat al-'Iraq al-Islamiyya, or ISI) was established on 15 October 2006.[3] Within ISI, al-Qaeda in Iraq was the largest group.[4] In October 2007, 23 groups came together to form the Supreme Command for Jihad and Liberation, led by former Iraqi Vice President and Deputy Chairman of the Iraqi Revolutionary Command Council, Izzat Ibrahim ad-Douri.[5] The Sunni nationalists and Islamists feared the

Shia-dominated government of Iraq. The threat groups, including offshoots of the Baath Party such as Jaysh al Fatih or Al Fatih Army, have assumed an outward Islamic character.[6] The Shia groups fought both the Sunni groups and the US-led coalition.[7] Two dozen well-structured groups worked with nearly 100 small-to-medium groups to make Iraq the most violent conflict in the world. The insurgency peaked in 2006–2007, and declined thereafter. US military estimates ranged from 8,000 to 20,000, although Iraqi intelligence officials have issued figures as high as 40,000 fighters plus another 160,000 supporters.[8] At the height of the insurgency in Iraq, the most lethal threat groups were al-Qaeda in Iraq which had a numerical strength of 2,000–3,500, and Ansar al Islam with 3,000–4,000 fighters. Of the nearly 100 threat groups, al-Qaeda in Iraq and Ansar al Islam belong to the strain of groups that are the most ideologically resilient, experienced, and networked. They are likely to last long after the other groups have been dismantled or have abandoned violence. This study traces the origins, development, and international linkages of these two most significant threat groups in Iraq during the Saddam and the post-Saddam periods, and assesses their likely impact (see Figure 1).

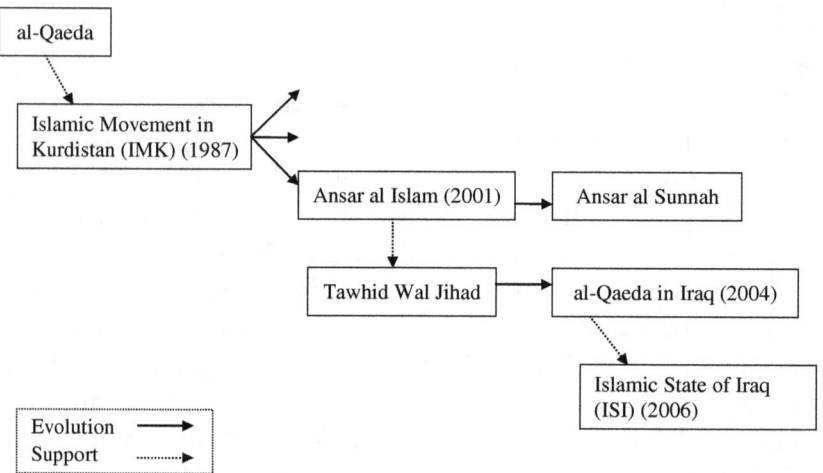

**Figure 1.** Evolution of al-Qaeda–linked groups in Iraq

## Background

Kurdish Islamism emerged as a response to Saddam's dictatorship that discriminated against and persecuted the Kurds. During the anti-Soviet, multinational Afghan Mujahidin campaign (1979–1989), the Kurdish Islamists from Iraq established links with foreign fighters in Afghanistan. Their natural points of contact and interface were with Afghan and Pakistani groups as well as with the Arab groups. The Kurdish Islamists worked with Abdul Rabi Rasul Sayyaf's Ittehad-e Islami bara-ye Azadi-ye Afghanistan formed in 1981, and with Abdullah Azzam's Maktab-il-khidamat (MaK: Afghan Service Bureau) formed in 1984.[9] Educated in the Middle East, unlike the other Afghan commanders, Sayyaf worked closely with the Arabs and other foreign fighters including the Kurds. This included Nashwan Abdulrazaq Abdulbaqi alias Abdal Hadi al Iraqi from Mosul, a former Major of Saddam's army.[10] Abdal Hadi gave up his Baathist leanings and joined the mujahidin fighting the Soviet Army in Afghanistan during the late 1980s. He served as an instructor in Sayyaf's Sadda camp in Pakistan. While many such as Abdal Hadi remained to serve the cause in Afghanistan, others returned home to serve the Islamist movements in their own countries.[11] Najmeddin Faraj Ahmad alias Mullah Mustapha Krekar (a Kurd from the Iraqi province of Al Sulaymaniyah) studied jurisprudence under Azzam. As MaK evolved into al-Qaeda, Azzam's deputy and successor Osama bin Laden took over the leadership.[12] Although the leadership of al-Qaeda was Arab during the formative years, the group established links with both Arab and non-Arab Muslim groups fighting both Muslim and non-Muslim regimes worldwide.

After the Soviets withdrew from Afghanistan in February 1989, a few thousand foreigners remained on the Afghanistan–Pakistan border. Those remaining in the area of Pakistan and Afghanistan included "5,000 Saudis, 3,000 Yemenis, 2,000 Egyptians, 2,800 Algerians, 400 Tunisians, 370 Iraqis, 200 Libyans and scores of Jordanians…"[13] Among the Iraqis, only a few joined al-Qaeda. After serving with Sayyaf to fight the Soviets, Abdal Hadi al Iraqi joined al-Qaeda, trained and dispatched fighters (including dispatches to Chechnya), contributed to the Encyclopedia of the Jihad, and rose within al-Qaeda's hierarchy to later become the head of al-Qaeda's military forces in the Kabul area.[14] He would go on to join al-Qaeda's Majlis Shura (consultative council), its highest decision-making body. As a Kurd, he was the only non-Arab to serve on al-Qaeda's apex council. After marrying a local woman who gave him a son, Abdal Hadi settled down in Peshawar and later in Kabul, where he maintained links with both the Iraqi Sunnis and the Iraqi Kurds.

A multinational group, al-Qaeda historically resided in non-Arab lands[15] and operated in both Arab and non-Arab lands.[16] After al-Qaeda relocated to Khartoum, Sudan in 1991, an al-Qaeda instructor visited northern Iraq and trained the IMK. The training course conducted in 1992 was the first known formal contact between al-Qaeda and IMK. The links between al-Qaeda and IMK persisted throughout the 1990s. Intermittently, both Iraqi Sunnis and Iraqi Kurds traveled to Pakistan to either train with or join al-Qaeda and the Taliban to fight against the Northern Alliance. As one of the commanders in the frontline, Abdal Hadi al Iraqi commanded 200 Afghans, Arabs, and other foreigners including Iraqi Sunnis and Iraqi Kurds.[17] Contact between northern Iraq and al-Qaeda took many facets. Through delegations and individuals that visited with Osama bin Laden, IMK dispatched videos of the atrocities committed by Saddam in the north of Iraq and of the suffering of the Kurds.[18]

After al-Qaeda's attacks on America's iconic landmarks on 11 September 2001, the ideological and operational links between the Kurdish Islamists and al-Qaeda grew. After the US coalition intervention in Afghanistan in October 2001, a segment of the al-Qaeda leadership moved to tribal Pakistan and to Iran.[19] Under international pressure, the Iranian government began to crackdown on the al-Qaeda presence in Iran. A few hundred foreign fighters including al-Qaeda members then moved through Iran and settled in northern Iraq, a safe haven from Saddam Hussein's atrocities established by the West. Although the global footprint of al-Qaeda included Iraq, the Kurdish Islamist groups were opposed to Saddam. If not for that safe haven, established north of Iraq's 36th parallel after the Gulf War in April 1991, Saddam's military would have dismantled the Islamist groups.[20]

## The Case Against Iraq

Even before 11 September 2001, the political leadership of the US was keen to invade Iraq. The US intelligence community actively looked for links between al-Qaeda and Saddam, as well as between Saddam and weapons of mass destruction (WMDs). However, they could find none that were credible.[21] Saddam's security services dispatched serving Iraqi intelligence officers to join Islamist groups to report back on their plans and preparations. As the US lacked an understanding of the threat groups, it misconstrued the presence of these former and serving intelligence operatives within the Islamist groups as Saddam's links to al-Qaeda. To justify the invasion of Iraq, the White House influenced the assessments of the US intelligence community. At least a segment of the international intelligence community still believes that Saddam worked with al-Qaeda and its associate groups in Iraq.[22] Addressing the UN Security Council on the US case against Iraq on 5 February 2003, the US Secretary of State Colin Powell said: "But what I want to bring to your attention today is the potentially much more sinister nexus between Iraq and the al-Qaeda terrorist network, a nexus that combines classic terrorist organizations and modern methods of murder. Iraq today harbors a deadly terrorist network headed by Abu Musab Zarqawi, an associate and collaborator of Osama bin Laden and his al-Qaeda lieutenants. ...We are not surprised that Iraq is harboring Zarqawi and his subordinates. This understanding builds on decades long experience with respect to ties between Iraq and al-Qaeda."[23] The misinterpretation of intelligence and the lack of understanding of the Middle East led the Bush administration to invade Iraq — an event that compounded the global threat.

Immediately after Powell at the UN referred to a facility manufacturing poisons and explosives in Khurmal, Ansar al Islam fi Kurdistan (Supporters of Islam in Kurdistan) invited journalists to visit and inspect the camp on 5 February 2003.[24] It is very likely that the facility was used to experiment and train in the use of cyanide, ricin and other poisons.[25] Commonly known as Ansar, the al-Qaeda–supported Kurdish Salafi group operated against both Kurdish secular groups and Saddam's regime. Even an International Crisis

Group (ICG) report noted that there is little independent evidence of links between Ansar al Islam and Baghdad.²⁶ ICG judged that it would be very hard for people or military supplies to pass between Baghdad and the Ansar enclave because a secular Kurdish group hostile to both of them controlled all the routes between them.²⁷

The US believed that Ansar al Islam played a key role in linking Osama bin Laden's al-Qaeda network with the Iraqi government. However, this was not true. When the US forces invaded Iraq, they were under the impression that Ansar was working with Saddam and that CBRN could be used against them. In an attempt to build the case for the invasion of Iraq, the US political leadership used counter-terrorism intelligence that was questionable and uncorroborated. This included the debriefing of Abd al-Hamid al-Fakhiri alias Ibn al-Shaykh al-Libi, the Internal Emir of Khalden Camp in Afghanistan, who was captured by the Pakistani government in early 2002. Although Ibn al-Shaykh was not an al-Qaeda member, together with Abu Zubaidah, the External Emir of Khalden Camp, he had worked with al-Qaeda after their camp was shut down in 1999. As the CIA believed him to be uncooperative, they flew him to Egypt. The revelations by Ibn al-Shaykh contributed appreciably, if not totally, to the justifications that led to the US decision to invade Iraq. Although the CIA had assessed the revelations as unreliable just one month before,²⁸ Powell told the UN: "Al-Qaeda continues to have a deep interest in acquiring weapons of mass destruction. As with the story of Zarqawi and his network, I can trace the story of a senior terrorist operative telling how Iraq provided training in these weapons to al-Qaeda. Fortunately, this operative is now detained, and he has told his story."²⁹ After the US invasion, Ibn al-Shaykh recanted his claims of contact between al-Qaeda, Saddam's government, and the Iraqi training in WMDs provided to al-Qaeda. On 22 November 2003, the Egyptian service returned Ibn al-Shaykh to the CIA. In January 2004, after US interrogators presented Ibn al-Shaykh with new evidence from other detainees, he acknowledged that under torture in Egypt, he had deliberately misled interrogators[30]:

> This is the first report from Ibn al-Shaykh in which he claims Iraq assisted al-Qaida's CBRN efforts. However, he lacks specific details on the Iraqi's

[sic] involved, the CBRN materials associated with the assistance, and the location where training occurred. It is possible he does not know any further details; it is more likely this individual is intentionally misleading the debriefers. Ibn al-Shaykh has been undergoing debriefs for several weeks and may describing [sic] scenarios to the debriefers that he knows will retain their interest… Saddam's regime is intensely secular and is wary of Islamic revolutionary movements. Moreover, Baghdad is unlikely to provide assistance to a group it cannot control.[31]

On 27 January 2005, President Bush said, "torture is never acceptable, nor do we hand over people to countries that do torture."[32] Nonetheless, what happened was far from the US government's stated policy. Under torture, detainees and inmates say what interrogators want to hear. Ibn al-Shaykh was no exception.

## Origins and Development of Threat Groups

Poor governance led to the emergence of Kurdist separatist and subsequently Islamist groups in the 1980s. During the Iran–Iraq war from September 1980 to August 1988, a segment of the Kurds in the north of Iraq did not support Saddam Hussein, the then ruler of Iraq. In response to the rebellion in Kurdistan, Saddam Hussein launched al Anfal, a campaign in the Iraqi Kurdistan beginning in 1986. Kurdish Islamists from Iraq gathered in Dizly, Iran to form the Islamic Movement in Kurdistan (IMK) in 1987. Together with his brothers, Ali, Osman, Sadik and Omar, Osman Abdul Aziz founded it. A towering figure, Osman was also joined by Ahmed Kaka Mohamed, Sheikh Mohamed Barzinjy, Ali Papier and other leaders. Iran's Ministry of Intelligence and National Security (known as Etelaat) supported IMK at its formation. Saddam's campaign, resulting in the death of 30,000 Kurds in Iraq's Kurdish north, lasted from 1986–1989. It included the use of chemical agents. The worst incident that occurred was from 16–17 March 1988 in Halabja, a town in the Sulaymaniyah Governorate, located about 10 miles from the Iranian border.

Kurdish Islamists benefited not only from Iran but also from the developments in Afghanistan. Several dozen Kurds traveled to Pakistan and fought against the Soviets throughout the 1980s, and beginning in 1988 both leaders and members of the IMK traveled to Peshawar. Initially they sided with the Arabs, but subsequently they formed Darul Akrad or the House of Kurds. Eight Kurds were killed in the fighting against the Soviets.[33] The most prominent leaders were Mullah Krekar, Abu Abdallah al Shafi'i alias Warba Holiri al-Kurdi, Azo Hawleri, Ayyub Afghani, and Omar Baziany.[34] Without exception, they all became significant leaders in Kurdish Islamist movements in the next decade. Together with the Afghan veterans, IMK members were determined to fight the Saddam regime. Supported by Etelaat, IMK entered Iraq in 1989 and relocated itself in Halabja. IMK leaders exercised their influence by preaching jihad, showing photos and screening videos of their experience in Afghanistan, and recruiting members, supporters and sympathizers to their movement. They claimed that "Allah succeeded us" and trained them to fight the way they did in Afghanistan.[35] After recruiting several hundred Kurds in mosques, they fought against Saddam's rule beginning in 1990. In 1991, uprising against Saddam, IMK joined the Patriotic Union of Kurdistan (PUK), the Kurdistan Democratic Party (KDP), and other Kurdish secular groups. But the unity among these rival groups was short-lived. With the Kurdish returnees from Afghanistan and Pakistan joining IMK, a faction of the IMK adopted the ideology of jihad as a strategy. After the IMK's Afghan veterans began to exercise their practice on the population, tensions emerged between the secular KDP and PUK with the IMK.

Between 1993 and 1994, IMK's extremists began to spread their influence in Irbil, Halabja, and Sulaimanya. One of their first acts included bombing a barbershop and throwing acid on the legs of the lady who had had a haircut there. Gradually, IMK's extremists came into conflict with PUK and KDP. Starting in 1994, PUK and IMK clashed, and PUK with the help of KDP killed a few hundred members of IMK. Furthermore, disagreements developed within IMK, and IMK split into several factions. Mullah Krekar, who was closest to Osama bin Laden, formed Salafia; Jihadiya was formed by Ali Abdul Aziz, who had the loyalty of many tribes; Omar Baziany and Mohomed Sofi formed Kurdish Hamas[36]; while Ali Papier wanted to be the leader of the IMK.

Like other Kurdish groups opposed to Saddam, IMK too received US assistance.[37] Over time, IMK suffered splits under the leadership of Shaykh Ali Abdul Aziz, the brother of the movement's founder. The year 2001 was decisive for the threat groups globally, including those in Kurdistan. In July 2001, IMK splinters — Kurdish Hamas and al Tawhid (Islamic Unification Movement, or IUM) — joined to form the Islamic Unity Front (IUF). In August, Second Soran Forces, another IMK splinter, joined them. After IUF was dissolved in early September 2001, Jund al Islam (Soldiers of Islam) was established on 1 September 2001. Under the leadership of Abdullah al-Shafi'i alias Mullah Wuria Hawleri, an Iraqi Kurd from the village of Gwer near Irbil, Jund al Islam evolved into Ansar al Islam on 12 December 2001. Mullah Krekar, who joined Ansar al Islam shortly after 9/11, later replaced Abu Abdullah Shafi'i as leader, while Shafi'i (who had also trained in Afghanistan) became Ansar's deputy leader.[38] Assad Mohammad Hassan alias Hawleri, formerly the leader of the Second Soran Unit, became Shafa's deputy. Abu Abdul Rahman, an Afghan-trained explosives expert, was also a founding member of Ansar. Before Abdul Rahman was killed in fighting in October 2001, he trained a number of fighters including Kurds. Ayyub Afghani, the Chief of Ansar's Media Bureau, was another explosives expert who had previously fought in Afghanistan.

Both IMK and its splinters were operating between Halabja and Hawraman, at the border of Iran and Iraq. Jund al Islam (the precursor of Ansar) assassinated Franso Hariri, a Christian Kurd and a senior official of the KDP, on 18 February 2001. In the wake of 9/11, Jund al Islam took hold of a swath of territory in northeastern Iraq, along the Iranian border. After suffering defeat by the PUK in December 2001, Jund al Islam was reconstituted as Ansar al Islam. Ansar established itself in an enclave in northeastern Iraq, on the strategic Shinirwe Mountain overlooking the town of Halabja, near the porous border with Iran — an area outside of Saddam Hussein's control. After its establishment, the group also seized the border town of Tawella, as well as the villages of Mila Chinara, Khak Kelan, Kharpan, Zardalhala, Hanadi, Dargashikhan, Balkha, Mishla, and Palyanaw. Over time, it expanded its influence by engaging PUK, the established power in the region.

Located near the villages of Biyara and Tawella, northeast of Halabja in the Hawraman region of Sulaymaniyah Province, Ansar al Islam fought PUK, the *de facto* ruling power in the region. After relocating to Iraq, Ansar al Islam controlled "a string of villages in the plains and mountains between the town of Halabja and the mountain ridge which marks Iraq's border with Iran... The area has been dubbed 'Iraq's Tora Bora' by some locals after the al-Qaeda stronghold in Afghanistan."[39] In September 2001, Ansar al Islam committed its worst atrocity in the village of Khela Hama, near Halabja, when it captured and massacred 42 members of PUK, which controlled the eastern half of Iraqi Kurdistan. Ansar al Islam killed leaders, bombed restaurants and desecrated Sufi shrines. Then in December, Ansar al Islam killed 103 members of PUK and injured 117 others who were returning home to celebrate the end of Ramadan. The pictures of the killings were placed on the Internet.[40]

In April 2002, Ansar attempted to kill Prime Minister Burham Salih, the head of the PUK-led Iraqi Kurdistan regional government. The attack, in which five of Salih's bodyguards were killed, was most likely ordered by Ahmed Fadil Nazal al-Khalayleh alias Abu Musab al Zarqawi. Starting early 2002, al-Qaeda members including Abu Musab, who relocated from Afghanistan, influenced both the *modus operandi* and the targeting strategy of Ansar. In July 2002, Ansar desecrated tombs of the Naqshbandi (Sufi) order. A tolerant Kurdish society condemned this act. On 10 February 2003, Ansar assassinated Shawkat Hajji Mushir (a founding member of PUK and a member of the Kurdish parliament) as well as two other Kurdish officials, who were under the belief that they were meeting with Ansar to negotiate as a substantial number of Ansar members allegedly wanted to defect. It was, however, a trap. Kurdistan experienced its first suicide bomb attack on 26 February 2003, when an Ansar suicide bomber used a Land Rover taxi (that regularly plied the route between Halabja and the town of Sayyid Sadiq) to help him cross from Ansar-held territory into the zone controlled by government forces.[41] Ansar had received the expertise to build car bombs from al-Qaeda. When confronted by government troops at a roadside checkpoint, the suicide bomber killed two soldiers, the taxi driver and himself. The attack coincided with a conference of Iraqi opposition organizations on a post-Saddam political order, attended by Zalmay Khalilzad, President Bush's special envoy to the Iraqi opposition.[42] It is very likely that the attacker wanted to target the meeting. From this attack, it was clear that Ansar would become the most threatening terrorist group to the coalition forces in Iraq.

## The Threat Landscape

Prior to invasion, the Western security and intelligence services, working with KDP and PUK, invested significant resources to develop intelligence on the threat groups in Iraq. An estimated 300–400 Iraqi Kurds were joined by 200–300 Arabs and other fighters that fled Afghanistan after the US-led coalition intervention in Afghanistan.[43] Their leader, Mullah Krekar, was host to a few hundred Arabs including Abu Musab al Zarqawi, who ran a training camp in Herat in Afghanistan near the Iranian border. With financial support from al-Qaeda, Abu Musab from Zarqa in Jordan established links with groups and individuals in the Levant. Most of the recruits of Abu Musab's group Tawhid Wal Jihad were from the Levant, including those living in Europe. Abu Musab, who was close to the al-Qaeda leadership, especially to Osama bin Laden and Dr. Ayman al Zawahiri (after the death of the al-Qaeda military commander Abu Haf alias Mohamed Atef), fled to Iran in late 2001. After the Iranians briefly detained Abu Musab, he relocated to Iraq in the late summer of 2002. Abu Musab's host, Mullah Krekar, opposed unity moves by the parent IMK to join PUK and work with the US in order to create an autonomous Kurdish state in the north of Iraq. Driven by the ideology of al-Qaeda, Mullah Krekar and his followers initially wanted to create an Islamic state in the north of Iraq and subsequently in the rest of Iraq.

With the help of Ansar al Islam, Abu Musab settled in Halabja and established training facilities in the northern Kurdish areas outside Saddam-controlled Iraq. Benefiting from the protection of the US northern No-Fly Zone, Abu Musab replicated the camp in Herat where training was imparted in regards to poison (especially ricin) and explosives, his favored weapon. In addition to building a vast network in the Levant and in Europe,[44] Abu Musab conducted operations in Iraq, Saudi Arabia, Syria, Lebanon, and Jordan, his own country of birth.[45] A regional terrorist, Abu Musab traveled personally, establishing various networks including a chemical attack in Jordan that would have killed several tens of thousands of people.[46] In May 2002, Abu Musab arrived in Baghdad for medical treatment and remained in the capital of Iraq for two months.[47] Western intelligence services assumed that Saddam "must have" collaborated with regards to Abu Musab's arrival or must have at least "known"[48] about it. However, Saddam did not know about it.

At the time of the US-led coalition intervention in Iraq in March 2003, there were multiple threat groups. The north of Iraq had emerged as an important safe haven for a few threat groups, both domestic and foreign. Ansar al Islam, which has links to al-Qaeda and other Arab threat groups from Afghanistan, was the most structured terrorist group. Ansar al Islam controlled Beriya, a tiny pocket of territory between Halabja and the Iranian border, an area about 80 kilometers (50 miles) southeast of the PUK's administrative center of Suleimaniya.[49] An associate group of al-Qaeda, Ansar al Islam was the host to Tawhid Wal Jihad led by Abu Musab al Zarqawi. Tawhid Wal Jihad relocated to Iraq from Afghanistan after the US intervention in 2001. Starting in 1999, Abu Musab al Zarqawi trained volunteers from Lebanon, Syria, Jordan, and Palestine. The volunteers therefore also worked closely with Ansar al Islam, which modeled itself on the Afghan Taliban.

During the US-driven invasion of Iraq, the first series of terrorist camps targeted belonged to Ansar al Islam. At that time, the US believed that the camps were trying to develop crude chemical weapons and had links to both Osama bin Laden's al-Qaeda and Saddam Hussein's regime. US Special Forces and air strikes supported by the PUK, a US ally, attacked Ansar al Islam hideouts. US Tomahawk cruise missiles and warplanes from the Red Sea hit Khurmal as well as six mountain villages in northern Iraq on 21 March 2003.[50] With the exception of Abu Taisir al Urdani, a specialist on poisons and Abu Musab's representative in northern Iraq, the strike failed to kill anyone of note. Nevertheless, it is likely that more than 100 Ansar al Islam members perished in the strike, and significant documents including foreign passports and training manuals were recovered.⁵¹ In a message "to the Muslims of Kurdistan, Iraq and the world," Ansar al Islam leader Abu Abdullah al Shafi'i threatened "martyrdom operations (suicide attacks) against the American and British Crusader forces."⁵² The document claimed that "more than 300 martyrdom fighters have renewed their devotion to God" ahead of suicide attacks.⁵³ "We will make Iraq a cemetery for the Crusaders and their servile agents," it said.⁵⁴ Most of Ansar's fighters dispersed to Iran and regrouped on the border. Some Ansar al Islam leaders, such as Abu Abdullah al Shafi'i, Ayyub Afghani, and Sa'adoon Mohammed Abdul Latif alias Abu Wa'il, were seen in the Iranian border city of Sanandaj in June and July 2003, regrouping their fighters and recruiting new men.⁵⁵

The US also targeted a lesser-known group, Komala, also in Khurmal. The leaders of Komala, in particular Sheikh Mohamed Barzinjy and Ali Papier (first leader of Komala), had good relations with Iran. They also had representation in the PUK-led Kurdish administration. The simultaneous attack targeting the political headquarters of Komala killed 60 members and injured another 50 members.⁵⁶ Although Komala, a moderate Islamic political group, was a part of the coalition Kurdish regional government, it also had friendly relations with Ansar.⁵⁷ Best practice dictates division of threat groups and pitching them against each other. When the US decision to target Komala was questioned, the US defended its position by stating that it had found links between Ansar and Komala. It is very likely that such links did exist.

## Ansar al Islam fi Kurdistan (Ansar al Islam)

Since its very inception, Ansar al Islam has operated with experienced Kurdish and foreign fighters. With the aim of creating an Islamic state, Ansar al Islam responded to the US-led invasion by mounting attacks against Western, Iraqi and Kurdish government targets as well as foreign contractors, starting in the Kurdish areas. On 22 March 2003, at the crossroads checkpoint outside the village of Khurmal, a suicide car bomb detonated, killing Australian journalist Paul Moran, four Kurds, and injuring dozens of other Kurdish peshmerga and civilians, including correspondent Eric Campbell.[58] The bomber's name was Abu Hur.[59] The spiritual leader of Ansar al Islam, Mullah Krekar (in Norway), justified the attack.[60] Then on 9 September 2003, three people were killed during an attempt to bomb a US Department of Defense office in Irbil. As a group of Kurds operating with foreigners, Ansar al Islam's operations were initially limited to the north.

As Ansar al Islam wished to operate in the rest of Iraq too, Ansar al Islam fi Kurdistan changed its official name to Ansar al Sunnah (Supporters of the Tradition) on 20 September 2003. Ansar recruited Sunni Arabs in central Iraq to join the largely Kurdish group from the north of Iraq. Influenced by the Arabs that fought in Afghanistan, particularly Tawhid Wal Jihad, Ansar al Sunnah conducted graphic beheadings. In October 2004, Ansar al Sunnah released a video beheading of a Turkish truck driver on its website. The kidnappers on the video identified themselves as members of Tawhid Wal Jihad, the al-Qaeda affiliate group led by Abu Musab. Ansar's other tactics included vehicle- and human-borne suicide attacks, abductions, assassinations, improvised explosive device attacks, rocket and mortar attacks, and roadside bombings. In October 2003, the Pentagon declared that Ansar al Islam had become the principal "terrorist adversary" of US forces in Iraq. As Ansar started to operate in central Iraq, including Baghdad, Ansar fighters were divided into six battalions: Nasr, Fat'h, Badr, Quds, Fida'iyun, and Salahuddin. Ansar fought within the "Sunni Triangle," north and west of Baghdad — the main battleground between US troops and insurgents.

Tawhid Wal Jihad, operationally close to al-Qaeda, influenced Ansar's operational outlook in that Ansar was focused on conducting high-profile attacks on symbolic and strategic targets, inflicting mass casualties and fatalities. In November 2003, Italian intelligence reported that an Ansar al Islam member helped organize the truck bombings of the headquarters of the Italian military contingent in Nasariyah, southern Iraq. On 1 February 2004, Ansar's suicide bombers hit *Eid* celebrations by PUK and KDP in Irbil, killing 109 and wounding 200. Ansar al Sunnah stated that the attack was in support of "our brothers in Ansar al Islam." Both Ansar and Tawhid Wal

Jihad vied for recognition by al-Qaeda. With al-Qaeda recognizing Tawhid Wal Jihad as a part of al-Qaeda, Abu Musab renamed his group "al-Qaeda in Iraq" in October 2004.

Due to the mounting daily killings of Shia Iraqis by al-Qaeda in Iraq in September 2005, disagreements between al-Qaeda in Iraq and Ansar developed, leading to a split in their alliance. Although al-Qaeda in Iraq and its former host, Ansar al Islam, started operating independently, Ansar maintained direct contact and communications with al-Qaeda. An Ansar leader, Abbas bin Farnas bin Qafqas alias Ali Wali, communicated with al-Qaeda leaders in Pakistan during 2005. However, Ali Wali was killed during a counterterrorism raid in Baghdad in May 2006.[61] In July 2007, Ansar al Sunnah was instrumental in forming an alliance of seven Sunni groups to prepare for the withdrawal of American and allied forces. In December 2007, Ansar al Sunnah formally acknowledged being derived from the Ansar al Islam.

Although over a hundred large-to-small threat groups emerged in Iraq during the US-led invasion, Ansar and al-Qaeda in Iraq were the two groups that posed the biggest threat. Under the influence of al-Qaeda, they favored suicide attacks against high-profile, strategic and symbolic targets. As most of their attacks were spectacular, they influenced the tempo of battle in Iraq and even inspired threat groups in the region and beyond.

## Tanzim Qaedat fi Bilad al-Rafidayn (al-Qaeda in Iraq)

In October 2004, Tawhid Wal Jihad renamed itself Tanzim Qaedat fi Bilad al-Rafidayn or al-Qaeda Organization in the Land of the Two Rivers, commonly known as al-Qaeda in Iraq.[62] After Tawhid Wal Jihad severed its ties with Ansar, the group came under the greater influence of al-Qaeda led by Osama. Under Abu Musab's leadership, al-Qaeda in Iraq emerged as the most violent terrorist group in the world. The US even offered a reward of US$25 million for information leading to Abu Musab's death or capture, the highest reward offered for a terrorist.

At its peak in 2006, the total number of al-Qaeda in Iraq combatants ranged between 2,000 and 3,500. It is responsible for most suicide attacks and generally the most spectacular attacks in Iraq.[63] Although 90% of the group was Iraqi by 2006, foreigners constituted about 90% of its suicide bombers. The key strength of al-Qaeda in Iraq was the Majlis al-Shurra Mujahidin fi al-Iraq — the Mujahidin Shura Council (MSC) of Iraq — an umbrella organization of eight groups with "al-Qaeda in Iraq" at its core.[64] However, MSC came under criticism from al-Qaeda in Iraq as the Council had to seek permission from other members before conducting certain operations.[65] The MSC, which was created in January 2006, was later replaced by the Hilf Mutayyabin (The Alliance of the Scented Ones).[66] On 15 October 2006, al-Qaeda established the Islamic State of Iraq (ISI) and calibrated it to serve the interests of al-Qaeda in Iraq. Twelve smaller militant groups in addition to al-Qaeda in Iraq operated within the structures of the ISI.[67] ISI received praise from al-Qaeda's leadership in Pakistan.[68]

Apart from attacking Coalition and Iraqi security forces, al-Qaeda in Iraq also has a confrontational policy against civilian Shi'ites and Iraqi nationalist resistance groups. Al-Qaeda's leadership discouraged Abu Musab's actions, but he refused to change his course. Although the orientation has changed since Abu Musab's tenure, the organization is still executing the same massacres now as it did during his tenure and it remains generally disliked among other militant groups in Iraq. These other militant groups have on many occasions appealed to Osama bin Laden for him to reel in al-Qaeda in Iraq. However, al-Qaeda's leadership has instead supported the unpopular establishment of Dawlat al-Iraq al-Islamiyah (The Islamic State of Iraq: ISI), which has tried to entice and coerce other militant groups to join in.

Al-Qaeda in Iraq focused mainly on vehicle- and human-borne suicide attacks. The group also improvised explosive device attacks, car bombings, and roadside bombings. After forming an alliance with Sunni groups, al-Qaeda in Iraq formed the ISI. However, the sheer scale of violence unleashed by al-Qaeda in Iraq did not go down well with the Iraqis. With members of the public providing intelligence on al-Qaeda in Iraq to the government and to the US, the group suffered the loss of its key leaders. This led to the steadfast degradation of the organization, starting with the capture of Abu Musab's deputy,

Hassan Mahmud Abu Nabha alias Milad al-Lubnani, in Lebanon in January 2006. Other key arrests led to intelligence culminating in Abu Musab's death in Baquba, Iraq on 7 June 2006.[69] At the time of Abu Musab's death, the insurgency in Iraq was at its peak and it continued at that pace for another year. His successor, Abd-al Munim Izzidine Ali Ismail alias Abu Hamza al-Muhajir alias Abu Ayyub al-Masri, was from the Egyptian Islamic Jihad, a group led by Dr. Ayman al Zawahiri that had merged with al-Qaeda.[70] A former instructor at the al-Faruq camp in Kandahar from 1999 to 2000, Abu Ayyub fled Afghanistan, relocated to Iran and was in Baghdad before the US invasion in 2003.[71] A founding member of Tawhid Wal Jihad, he became an instructor on the manufacture of improvises and facilitated the travel of foreign fighters to Baghdad.

After Abu Musab's death, Abu Ayyub pledged allegiance to Abu Umar al-Baghdadi, who was declared in November 2006 Amir al-Mu'minin (Leader of the Faithful) of the newly formed ISI.[72] Despite Abu Ayyub reaching out to the Iraqis and their groups, who were fighting the coalition and Iraqi forces, al-Qaeda in Iraq faced insurmountable challenges.[73] The backlash against Abu Musab's al-Qaeda in Iraq was the first permanent fracture within the insurgency. Although Abu Ayyub tried to appeal to the wider Iraqi population,[74] the previous massacres of tribal leaders and civilians had led to a deterioration of public support. The beginning of the decline of al-Qaeda in Iraq was the unity among Anbar's 25 tribes brought on by the high civilian casualties caused by attacks executed by al-Qaeda in Iraq. After questioning the authority and legitimacy of tribes in al-Anbar, an al-Qaeda in Iraq member said: "This tribal system is un-Islamic. We are proud to kill tribal leaders who are helping the Americans."[75] The tribal formations included Hamzah Brigade, created in 2004 and consisting mainly of the Albu-Mahal tribe from the al-Qaim area of al-Anbar province. The group has since been officially sanctioned by the Iraqi government under the name of Desert Protection Corps. Another tribal formation sprang forth in 2005 and was known as the Tribal Council. This Council was led by the powerful Albu-Fahad tribe, from Ar Ramadi. Unfortunately, this Council was severely weakened when "al-Qaeda in Iraq" killed the leader of the Council, Sheikh

Nasser Abdulkarim al-Miklaf, in January 2006. All of these tribal formations were based either on one single tribe or on the tribes around one town or city. Thus, due to their small and fragmented power bases, these tribal formations were usually defeated and their leaders often killed. However, this changed during the summer of 2006, when Majlis al-Shurra Inqath fi al-Anbar (The al-Anbar Salvation Council) was established. Eleven tribes, who took part in The Awakening of al-Anbar Conference, formed this Council. Each of the eleven tribes have their own armed formations, but combined, the Salvation Council claims to have a military force of 30,000 tribal fighters.[76] In September 2006, 51 tribal leaders from the Salvation Council, led by Al-Shaykh Abd-al-Sattar Buzay Abu-Rishah, met with Iraqi Prime Minister Nuri al-Maliki. The Salvation Council asked the Iraqi government for help in combating the terrorists (al-Qaeda in Iraq/MSC) in al-Anbar. Prior to this meeting, one of the main leaders of The al-Anbar Salvation Council, Sheikh Hamid Farhan, stated that the Council's military formations had killed five members of "al-Qaeda in Iraq," including the local leader in the town of Hit.[77]

Following this meeting, another clash occurred in November, when forces from the Salvation Council battled ISI (led by al-Qaeda in Iraq) near the town of Sofia in al-Anbar. The coalition forces assisted the tribal fighters with air and artillery strikes.[78] According to the leader of the Salvation Council, Al-Shaykh Abd-al-Sattar Buzay al-Rishawi, forces from the Salvation Council had raided an al-Qaeda in Iraq stronghold and killed 55 members, while losing nine of their own.[79] By mid-February 2007, the tribes of al-Anbar had contributed 2,400 individuals to the local police forces, and 1,600 members to a new tribal force called the Emergency Response Unit. The Emergency Response Unit received training from US forces in Iraq.[80] As of February 2007, the US cooperated with 12 tribes, up from three in June 2006.[81]

By February 2007, the Salvation Council had become such a threat to the forces of al-Qaeda in Iraq and ISI that the latter started a large terror campaign against the leaders, members and families of the al-Anbar Salvation Council. In the middle of February 2007, more than 20 mourners traveling from a funeral in Fallujah were pulled from their bus and killed, due to their alleged family ties with members of the Salvation Council. During the same period, two suicide bombers struck, respectively, the blast wall outside and the house of tribal leader, Al-Shaykh Abd-al-Sattar Buzay al-Rishawi, who leads the al-Anbar Salvation Council. Five police officers and six civilians were killed in the attack, but the main target escaped.[82] In late February 2007, a suicide bomber detonated his truck outside a Sunni mosque in the town of Habbaniyah in al-Anbar province, killing at least 39 people. The mosque was targeted because the Imam (prayer leader) of the mosque had spoken out against "extremists."[83]

The opponents of al-Qaeda in Iraq argue that al-Qaeda in Iraq is guilty of fratricide, and that its transnational goals in Iraq have endangered the Iraqi people. The Islamic Army of Iraq on 27 October 2007 claimed that al-Qaeda in Iraq "waged an attack in al-Shakhat [a part of al-Latifiyah] which resulted in the death of 4 unarmed citizens [as well as] an element of the Islamic Army with an insidious act and destroyed fourteen houses."[84] Starting in 2007, the rivalry steadily heightened. On 14 September 2007, al-Qaeda in Iraq claimed that Hamas in Iraq (a former faction of the 1920 Revolutionary Brigades) "worked hard to uncover the weapons of the mujahideen and stood side-by-side with the occupiers and fought us…"[85] However, Hamas in Iraq claimed that it "did not participate in any fight against the al-Qaeda network and will never, ever cooperate with the occupiers."[86] The accusations continued. On 4 January 2008, Hamas claimed: "al-Qaeda's fight against the resistance and mujahideen units … considered towards the benefit of the occupiers … put a drain on our youth and weaponry. The occupying forces were unable to enter Diyala until al-Qaeda paved the way for them by killing Sunnis and demolishing their homes, mosques, and hospitals … Several individuals from the Islamic State of Iraq are responsible for killing commanders and fighters from our brigades in the Diyala province … killed them and mutilated them … killed our men's wives and children."[87]

After the US reached out to the Iraqi Sunni groups, the al-Qaeda in Iraq's ISI began fighting the rival Sunni insurgent groups. These Sunni groups argued that al-Qaeda in Iraq had started to "terrorize the mujahidin under the pretext that their banners were agent banners, and it had the audacity to turn on the people of jihad and kill a number of the leaders of the Muslim Movement of the Mujahidin of Iraq, who, despite our reservations of them, should not be killed. They shot them in the back outside their homes, in their mosques, and amid their children."[88]

The main argument made by the rival Sunni groups was that al-Qaeda in Iraq had distorted the resistance by fomenting sectarian conflict. On 15 April 2008, the Army of al-Mustafa, a breakaway faction of the Islamic State of Iraq (ISI), claimed: "ISI threatened one of our field commanders with death for no apparent reason ... We see no justification for the acts carried out by the brothers from the ISI — they have blackmailed us, threatened us, and seized the assets of the Army of al-Mustafa."[89]

After Zarqawi's death, al-Qaeda in Iraq's ISI lost its strongholds in the Diyala and Salahadin provinces and in Kirkuk. Fighting continued in Nineveh, particularly in Mosul, between coalition and Sunni forces and the ISI. The attacks in Mosul in 2009 included operations that targeted US and Iraqi forces as well as militiamen of an Awakening council in Latifiyah, Babil province, as they waited to receive their salaries. The emergence of the Kurdistan Brigades demonstrated al-Qaeda in Iraq's ambition to establish a foothold in the Kurdish areas. Pledging their allegiance to Abu Omar al-Baghdadi, the leader of the ISI, a representative of the brigades said: "We are your brothers in the Kurdistan Brigades and we pledge our allegiance to the Islamic State of Iraq ... To the two Kurdish puppets, Jalal Talabani and Masud Barzani, I swear by God that we have no mercy or sympathy towards the traitors who sold themselves to the enemies of God. Your throats will be slit."[90]

The target of ISI's attacks shifted from coalition and Iraqi forces to the Awakening movement. This caused fear, opposition and revenge against al-Qaeda in Iraq's ISI. Due to declining support as well as increasing confrontations with the tribes of al-Anbar, the ISI moved most of its operations into the Baghdad and Diyala province. Especially in Diyala province, al-Qaeda in Iraq has received some positive responses to Abu Hamza al-Muhajir's outreach and reconciliation efforts between the tribes of Iraq and Muslim groups. On 4 October 2006, a statement from the Bubaz tribes referred directly to Abu Hamza's call for reconciliation, by declaring that "permanent reconciliation between the warring groups ... opens the field for the sons of the tribe to follow any faction or Jihadi brigade they wish to join in the quest for reward from Allah and destruction of the Crusader invade."[91]

In Diyala and Baghdad province, al-Qaeda in Iraq and especially the Iraqi Salafiyah groups like Jaish al-Islami have managed to draw some support from local Sunni Arabs. Local Sunni Arabs perceive these groups as their only guardians against the Shiite death squads, who have killed thousands. Despite these developments in Diyala and Baghdad, however, we assess that Abu Hamza al-Muhajir's outreach program has been an abject failure. The outreach program has not been able to woo major Iraqi resistance or militant Salafiyah movements into the ISI. Instead, actions on the ground by members of al-Qaeda in Iraq have further alienated these actors. Thus, despite his speeches and efforts at networking, Abu Hamza al-Muhajir has generally been unable to change the dynamics on the ground. Abu Musab's ideologically uncompromising legacy with its tit-for-tat cycle of revenge is still guiding the local al-Qaeda in Iraq leaders, members and supporters on the ground.

ISI remains active in the country; on 21 September 2009, it announced its second "cabinet" formation in a video released on jihadist forums. According to the SITE Intelligence Group, the video, produced by ISI's media arm, al-Furqan, features a spokesman for ISI's "Information Ministry" reading a statement from ISI leader Abu Omar al-Baghdadi that lists the ministerial positions. The statement also assures of the group's continued activity in jihad as the ISI enters its third year. ISI had previously announced its first "cabinet" formation in a video released on 19 April 2007, naming 10 individuals as "ministers." The new list consists of the following nine names:

- Sheikh Abu Hamza al-Muhajir — First Minister and Minister of War
- Sheikh Abdul Wahhab al-Mashadani — Minister of Shariah Affairs

- Sheikh Muhammad al-Duleimi — Minister of Public Relations
- Sheikh Hassan al-Jabouri — Minister of Martyr and Prisoner Affairs
- Sheikh Ustadh Abdul Razzaq al-Shemari — Minister of Security
- Sheikh Doctor Abdullah al-Qaysi — Minister of Health
- Sheikh Ustadh Ahmed al-Ta'i — Minister of Information
- Sheikh Engineer Usama al-Laheibi — Minister of Oil
- Sheikh Ustadh Yunis al-Hamadani — Minister of Finance

Despite the new "cabinet" and Abu Hamza's other efforts, al-Qaeda in Iraq remains a fringe group, far removed from the mainstream Sunni Iraqi militant groups. Although al-Qaeda in Iraq may find a significant base in the community if the coalition withdraws too rapidly, it faces mounting opposition from most Iraqi groups. Nonetheless, al-Qaeda in Iraq remains one of the largest and best-funded militant organizations in Iraq. The group remains at the center of the ISI and is the single most influential Sunni militant group in Iraq.

## Response

Since the US-led coalition invasion of Iraq in March 2003, the national, regional, and global threat landscape has altered dramatically. In late 2003, when the coalition forces failed to provide basic necessities like water and electricity to the public, the Iraqi insurgency took off. As US administrators failed to understand how best to manage Iraq and its people, the public turned against the occupation forces. Furthermore, the US made the strategic error of dismantling the Iraqi military. Public support for trained Iraqi militiamen led to a sustained insurgency. Beginning in late 2003, three clusters of threat groups emerged: pro–al-Qaeda groups, pro-Baathist groups, and pro-Iran groups. With the flow of foreign fighters, Iraq emerged as the most violent theater in 2004.

Erroneously, the US perceived the biggest threat to Iraq as coming from the Baathists and not from the militant Islamists. L. Paul Bremer, the head of the Coalition Provisional Authority who dismantled the Iraqi army, and the then National Security Advisor and former Secretary of State Condoleezza Rice failed to understand that the core threat stemmed from al-Qaeda in Iraq's ISI. While the White House and the State Department blamed Syria for the insurgency, the US military and the CIA knew the threat but lacked support to focus on the real enemy. Sheikh Talal al-Gaood, a Sunni businessman who died of heart disease in March of 2006, was enraged by the "endless mistakes" of the US leadership.[92] He said: "You [Americans] face a Wahhabi threat that you cannot even begin to fathom," and he derided White House "propaganda" about the role of Syria in fueling the insurgency.[93] When the US military wanted to co-opt the tribal leaders, the White House and State Department blocked it. The first round of talks started in August 2003, when tribal leaders met with US military officials in Jordan. A second round of talks took place in Anbar province in November 2004. Had the US politicians understood the importance of co-opting the tribal leaders in 2003 or 2004, the insurgency would not have escalated and led to the colossal loss of life and property.

The turning point of the insurgency occurred when Sunni tribal groups, led by tribal Sheikhs, united to form clusters to protect their tribes from al-Qaeda in Iraq's ISI. With the steady increase in violence in Iraq and no assistance from the Shia-dominated Baghdad government or from Washington, the Sunni tribes reached out to the US Marines for help. Although the US was reluctant to assist them initially, Colonel John Coleman, the chief of staff for the First Marine Expeditionary Force, disregarded Washington's advice. He went to Fallujah, a city in the heart of the Sunni triangle, to assist the call of the tribal leaders to fight al-Qaeda in Iraq after the killing of four US security contractors in April of 2004. A Saddam-lookalike former general and former Iraqi military personnel also turned up to help coalition forces in Fallujah.[94] Although the resistance from Washington to the US military co-opting tribal leaders remained, the model for collaboration between the US and the tribes was supported by Marine Lieutenant General James T. Conway, General David Petraeus, and Robert Gates, the Secretary of Defense. As US understanding of Iraqi nationalism grew, the US worked together with the Iraqi Sunni groups in its quest to defeat the ISI.

The tipping point arrived when the tribes started to receive financial support, political guidance, and military advice from the US. The US politico-military strategy paid dividends when the US started to work with Iraqi Sunni groups, thus dividing the potential and actual support base of ISI led by al-Qaeda in Iraq. After Fallujah, similar efforts sprang up among army units patrolling in Tel Afar and in Ramadi where, five months after Coleman's Fallujah initiative, American military officers began tentative approaches with the Rishawi tribe.[95] Despite the killing of Ramadi's Sheikh Abdul Sattar Abu Risha in a car bomb attack in September of 2007, the tribes' strategy spread and even took hold in Babil province's "Triangle of Death," the heavily fought-over area south of Baghdad.[96] Starting early 2007, the US alliance with Babil's leaders (former enemies) grew, and by May 2007 the Babil tribes received US funding including "$370 for each provincial policeman hired by Babil's Janabi tribe, a potent and influential force in southern and western Iraq."[97] When the Americans called for a meeting of the Awakening Councils with the Shia-dominated Iraqi government (which was skeptical of the tribes' US strategy officials) on 25 June 2007, a suicide bomber penetrated three levels of security and killed 12 Iraqis, including six key members of the Anbar Salvation Council.[98] Nevertheless, despite al-Qaeda in Iraq targeting several leaders and their families, the Awakening movements in Iraq made a difference.

As the linchpin of the American strategy to pacify Iraq, within a year of the formation of the Awakening movement, the strength of the groups grew to between 65,000–80,000 members.[99] The Sunni leaders organized pockets of resistance against al-Qaeda in Iraq and the ISI starting in Anbar province in 2005. This core was later joined by other Sunni groups that had previously worked with al-Qaeda in Iraq. These groups joined the core after realizing that al-Qaeda in Iraq did not have the interests of Iraq at heart. Although the "surge" helped in lowering violence, the Awakening movement that began in Anbar province and continued in Baghdad in 2008 was the "most significant reason for the decline."[100]

## Conclusion

The surge in troops and the Coalition and Iraqi forces working in partnership brought the grave situation in Iraq under control. This included the Shia groups, strong in the South, supported and guided by Iran. The largest Shia group, the Mahdi Army (a militia force created by the Iraqi Shia cleric Muqtada al-Sadr in June of 2003), remains a threat despite significant losses in major military battles. With US withdrawal, Iran is gradually influencing both the Shia government in Baghdad and the Shia population of Iraq. The US invasion of Iraq destabilized the entire region and allowed for the emergence of Iran as the dominant regional power. Iran has accelerated its nuclear weapons program, currently sponsors more terrorist and insurgent groups than ever before, and has become a crucial player in Iraq. Unless Iran is continuously engaged, the Middle East will remain the most unstable region in the foreseeable future.

The solution to the problem in Iraq came from the Iraqis themselves. In 2005 and 2006, the Iraqis became tired of the violence directed by al-Qaeda in Iraq against Iraqis. Nonetheless, their resentment against al-Qaeda in Iraq could be harnessed only after the US was convinced that a partnership with the Iraqi Sunni tribes was the only way to stabilize Iraq. With the appointment of Lt. General David Petraeus, a counter-insurgency specialist, as the Commanding General of Multinational Forces in Iraq in January 2007, the US strategy changed. Instead of conducting large-scale arrests, the kinetic operations became targeted. While using its force judiciously, the US built local security forces with its partners, rebuilt the utilities infrastructure, invested in the economy, and held elections reinvigorating the political process. More importantly, the US started to work with Sunni groups that had hitherto collaborated with al-Qaeda, and reduced violence in Iraq dramatically by 80% in 2007. A further surge of troops enabled the US to both contain and limit the influence of al-Qaeda and other violent groups.

By October 2008, when Petraeus (a visionary leader) handed over command in Iraq, the US had mastered Iraq. Together with a team of highly competent leaders, Petraeus had built governmental capacity, developed employment programs, and improved daily life for Iraqi citizens.[101] However, among the group of countries suffering from insurgency and terrorism, Iraq and Afghanistan continue to witness the highest levels of violence. As of 2009, the activities of Sunni and Shi'ite insurgent groups were largely limited to attacks against coalition and Iraqi forces in areas of central and northern Iraq. In addition to Shia and Sunni groups, nationalist insurgent groups also mounted attacks. For instance, the Army of the Men of al-Nakshabandia Way downed two US helicopters in Huweija district, Kirkuk province on 26 January 2009. Led by former Iraqi Vice President and Deputy Chairman of the Iraqi Revolutionary Command Council, Izzat Ibrahim al-Duri, Nakshabandia Army is one of 22 groups in the Supreme Council of Jihad and Liberation.[102] The threat of insurgency, especially of terrorism, is likely to remain a feature of Iraqi lives in the foreseeable future.

The formation, sustenance, and growth of existing as well as new threat groups in Iraq during invasion, occupation, and in the aftermath present a new and complex set of challenges for the international community. The threat groups in Iraq, especially the ones behind spectacular attacks, have influenced terrorist groups worldwide. Iraq has influenced the tempo, technology, and templates for attacks elsewhere. Similarly, developments outside Iraq have impacted on the threat groups in Iraq. For instance, the Israeli offensive in Gaza between 27 December 2008 and 18 January 2009 fostered amongst insurgents in Iraq a community supporting the besieged and attacked Palestinians. Several groups, such as the Mujahideen Army, Sa'ad bin Abi Waqqas Army, and Shield of Islam, launched campaigns in honor of Gazans, promising to escalate their attacks against US forces as a form of solidarity and support.[103]

Islamic Army in Iraq (IAI), Hamas-Iraq, JAMI, Mujahideen Army, and the Shariah Committee of Ansar al Sunnah came together for a joint project called "Campaign of the Iraqi Resistance in Support of Gaza." They claimed responsibility for several attacks in the beginning and middle of January 2009 against US forces in areas of Anbar, Baghdad, Kirkuk, and Salah al-Din provinces.[104] IAI and Hamas-Iraq also encouraged Muslim support for the Palestinian resistance, Hamas in particular. At the conclusion of the offensive in Gaza, the insurgent groups in Iraq congratulated the Palestinians for their endurance. The al-Qaeda–affiliated groups, the Islamic State of Iraq (ISI) and Ansar al Islam, also offered support, not through attack campaigns, but via incitement of Muslims everywhere to strike US, Israeli, and Arab interests.[105]

Iraq, a man-made disaster, will remain an important global center of terrorism in the years to come. Nonetheless, the US is a well-intentioned nation. It did not invade Iraq for oil or to secure a base for its forces. Neither did the US invade Iraq because it has a problem with Islam or with Muslims. In order to oust Saddam, a dictator, the US made a strategic miscalculation. Today, the US leaves behind a fragmented nation that is under-prepared to meet its security challenges. Despite the billions of dollars of investment and the colossal loss of lives, Iraq will remain an insecure environment. The US is engaged in a phased withdrawal from the country, at a time when Iraqi capacity is not adequately developed. While Iraq's neighbors will be able to manage the threat stemming from Iraq, the threat within Iraq to Iraqis will remain the most profound. If not the greatest challenge, one of the biggest challenges successive Iraqi governments will face in the coming decade will be to restore peace and security in Iraq. The threat to Iraq will stem not only from domestic but also from foreign terrorist groups, notably groups inspired and instigated by al-Qaeda and its associated groups. Like Afghanistan, Muslims worldwide radicalized by Iraq, and both Iraqi and foreign veterans of Iraq will remain a source of threat in Iraq and beyond. Good governance in Iraq, international economic development, and Iraq's ability and willingness to collaborate with the international security and intelligence community will be central in reducing and managing the threat.

The wave of global extremism spurred by the violence in Iraq will persist long after US withdrawal. In contrast to the Saddam Hussein era, Iraq in the post-Saddam era will witness sustained violence that will affect both the neighborhood and the world. In an earlier generation, the disastrous Soviet invasion of Afghanistan spawned an ideology and a pool of foreign fighters that continue to threaten international security. Likewise, the US invasion of Iraq has created a plethora of threat groups that will be a source of domestic, regional and global instability.

Although Obama is reaching out to the Muslims, he should tender an apology for his predecessor, President Bush. Despite claims by the Bush administration of association, the Muslim world generally did not believe that Saddam was flirting with al-Qaeda and its associated groups in the north of Iraq. Furthermore, the Muslim world did not believe in the US claim that Saddam was manufacturing WMDs. As the al-Qaeda and the WMD links have been disproved, the Muslim world continues to question the true US intention for invasion. Ideologues including the al-Qaeda leader in Saudi Arabia, Yousef al Ayeri, exploiting Muslim sentiments, called on Muslims worldwide to respond to the invasion. In "Crusader's War," an al-Qaeda blueprint for fighting in Iraq, Yousef al Ayeri said: "If democracy is established in Iraq, that will be the death of Islam." A proportion of Muslims worldwide perceived the invasion as an attack against Islam and Muslims, a theme propagated by al-Qaeda. Al-Qaeda, like-minded groups and their supporters will continue to highlight the Muslim suffering, resentment and anger in Iraq. The outlook of a significant segment of the Muslim population, especially in the Middle East, translates into anti-Americanism. A narrow segment of that population provides sympathy and support for terrorism and extremism. As a result, the ability of al-Qaeda and its associated groups to ideologically influence territorial and diaspora and migrant communities grows appreciably. The failure of the US to contain the violence in Iraq led not only to an expansion of influence by threat groups in Iraq, but also to an expansion of influence overseas. Benefiting from the sympathy and support accrued from the fallout of Iraq, al-Qaeda created a global movement.

Iraq also proved to be a huge distraction from hunting the true masterminds and supporters of the 9/11 attacks. While the US poured in resources to fight the threat groups in Iraq, including its limited specialist resources, al-Qaeda's senior leadership located in tribal Pakistan survived. The diversion of US resources to Iraq from 2003 until now has enabled both al-Qaeda and like-minded groups to make a strategic comeback. How will the phased US withdrawal in Iraq impact US strategy *vis-à-vis* its engagement in other theaters? With public opinion against the US, will a similar expedition result in reluctance on the part of the US government to intervene in other countries, including those that really need help? Will terrorist groups regard Iraq as a template to oust intervention forces? Taliban propaganda in 2009 focused on the new President of the United States, Barack Obama, and advised the US to withdraw from Afghanistan.[106] "The US," al-Qaeda projects, "will ultimately succumb to the same fate as the Soviet Union — collapse and removal from the global stage as a superpower — unless they draw lessons from the Soviet experience and reverse their military policy on Afghanistan."[107]

Both Abu Ayyub al-Masri alias Abu Hamza al-Muhajir (the leader of al-Qaeda in Iraq) and Hamid Dawud Mohamed Khalil al Zawi alias Abu Omar al-Qurashi al-Baghdadi (the leader of MSC) were killed on 18 April 2010. Nonetheless, the threat to Iraq from al-Qaeda in Iraq and its associated groups persists after Obama announced the official end of US combat operations in Iraq on 31 August 2010.

## Notes

1. The most prominent Sunni groups in Iraq were Salahudeen al-Ayyubi Brigades (JAAMI), Al-Fatihin Army, 1920s Revolution Brigades, Al-Qassas Brigade, Iraqi Jihad Union, Army of al-Mustafa, Dera Islam Brigade, Saad bin abi Waqqas Brigades, The Kurdistan Brigades, Al-Qaeda in Iraq, Army of the Victorious Sect, Army of Ahlus Sunnah wal Jamaah, Ansar al Islam, Islamic Army in Iraq, Mujahideen Army, Hamas of Iraq, and Al-Rashideen Army.
2. "Main Sunni Group Vows No Deal with US," *Agence France-Presse*, 7 January 2008.
3. Al-Qaeda in Iraq formed a coalition of Sunni groups that consisted of Jeish al-Fatiheen (Conquering Army), Jund al-Sahaba (Soldiers of the Sahaba), Katbiyan Ansar Al-Tawhid wal Sunnah (Brigades of Monotheism and Religious Conservatism), Jeish al-Taiifa al-Mansoura (Army of the Victorious Sect), Monotheism Supporters Brigades, Saray al-Jihad Group, al-Ghuraba Brigades, al-Ahwal Brigades, Jamaat Ansar al-Sunna (formerly Jaish Ansar al-Sunna, Ansar al-Islam), ar-Rayat as-Sawda (Black Banner Organization), Asaeb Ahl el-Iraq (Factions of the People of Iraq), Wakefulness and Holy War, Abu Theeb's group, and Jaish Abi Baker's group.
4. "Al-Muhajir Pledges Allegiance to Al-Baghdadi, Threatens US, Europe," Jihadist Websites — OSC Report, 11 November 2006. Although al-Qaeda in Iraq claimed its strength to be 12,000 fighters, its hardcore was a few thousand fighters.

5. The Command consisted of the Army of the Men of the Naqshbandi Order, The Army of the Prophet's Companions, The Army of the Murabiteen, The Army of al-Hamzah, The Army of the Message, The Army of Ibn al-Walid, The United Command of the Mujahideen in Iraq, The Liberation Brigades, The Army of al-Mustafa, The Army of the Liberation of Iraq, Squadrons of the Martyrs, The Army of the Sabireen, The Brigades of the Jihad in the Land of the Two Rivers, The Army of the Knight for the Liberation of the Self-Rule Area, Squadrons of the Jihad in Basra, Jihadist Squadrons of Fallujah, The Patriotic Popular Front for the Liberation of Iraq, The Squadrons of the Husayni Revolution of at-Taff, Squadrons of the Liberation of the South, Army of Haneen, Squadrons of Diyala for Jihad and Liberation, The Squadrons of Glory for the Liberation of Iraq, and Kurdistan Liberation Army.
6. The Baathist groups are: Fedayeen Saddam (Saddam's Men of Sacrifice), al-Awda (The Return), General Command of the Armed Forces, Resistance and Liberation in Iraq, Iraqi Popular Army, New Return, Patriotic Front, Jihaz al-Iilam al-Siasi lil hizb al-Baath (Political Media Organ of the Ba'ath Party), Popular Resistance for the Liberation of Iraq, and Al-Abud Network.
7. The Shia groups were Mahdi Army (Jaish-i-Mahdi); its faction, Abu Deraa; Badr Organization (Badr Brigade/Bader Corps), the armed wing of the Supreme Council for the Islamic Revolution in Iraq (SCIRI); Jund As-Samaa (Soldiers of Heaven/Supporters of the Mahdi); Asaeb Ahl Al-Haq (League of the Righteous People); and other special groups backed by Iran.
8. "Armed Groups in Iraq Guide," *BBC News*, 15 August 2006. The classified estimates reflect a similar range.
9. Interview, Abdul Rabi Rasul Sayyaf, Paghman, Afghanistan, 20 March 2008.
10. "Footage Showing al-Qaeda Leader in Afghanistan Abd al-Hadi al-Iraqi Downing an American Fighter Jet," Middle East Media Research Institute (MEMRI), 29 May 2005.
11. Sa'adoon Mohammed Abdul Latif alias Abu Wa'il, an Iraqi intelligence officer, also abandoned Saddam's service and visited Afghanistan in 1999. Eventually, he joined Ansar al Islam, the Kurdish Islamist group with links to al-Qaeda.

Terrorist Threat in Iraq: Origins, Development and Impact    141

12. Since the creation of al-Qaeda (The Base) in Peshawar, Pakistan on 18 August 1988, al-Qaeda has been led by Osama bin Laden, a former citizen of Saudi Arabia. Al-Qaeda founding documents recovered from Bosnia, ICPVTR Database, Singapore; Pervez Musharraf, *In the Line of Fire* (London: Simon and Schuster, 2006), p. 219; and Peter Bergen, *The Osama bin Laden I Know* (New York: Free Press, 2006), p. 80.
13. James Bruce, "Arab Veterans of the Afghan War," *Jane's Intelligence Review*, Vol. 7, No. 4 (1 April 1995), p. 175.
14. As a commander and accountant for al-Qaeda, Abdal Hadi ran both the al-Qaeda Army and maintained an office in the Ashara Guest House in Kart-E-Parwan province in Kabul, Afghanistan. Interrogations of Nurredin Nafei, Interrogation Report, Moroccan Justice Department 2003 and United States of America v. Abdul Zahir, 20 January 2006.
15. Al-Qaeda leadership relocated its headquarters from Pakistan to Sudan in 1991, and returned to Afghanistan in 1996. In Sudan, al-Qaeda was hosted by its spiritual leader Dr. Hasan al-Turabi and its ruler General Umar al-Bashir from 1991–1996, and in Afghanistan by its leader Mullah Umar from 1996–2001.
16. Al-Qaeda operated in Iraq, Chechnya, Algeria, Somalia, Saudi Arabia, Yemen, and a dozen other countries.
17. Mark Mazzetti and David Cloud, "CIA Held Qaeda Leader in Secret Jail for Months," *The New York Times*, 27 April 2007; and US Defense Department press release and bio of Abdal Hadi al Iraqi, released 27 April 2007.
18. Of the 250 videotapes recovered by CNN in Afghanistan, at least two tapes were IMK or pro-IMK. "Al-Qaeda Archive Uncovered," *BBC*, 19 August 2002; and "Tapes Give Evidence of al-Qaeda's Global Reach," *CNN*, 23 August 2002.
19. "Spy Chief Pushes for Action in Pakistan," *Associated Press*, 27 February 2007.
20. Chris Hedges, "The safe haven was patrolled by American, British and French warplanes based in Turkey: Baghdad's move puts the future of Kurdish safe haven in doubt," *New York Times*, 1 September 1996.
21. Bob Drogin, *Curveball: Spies, Lies, and the Man Behind Them: The Real Reason America Went to War in Iraq* (London: Ebury Press, 2007), p. 319; and Rohan Gunaratna, "Iraq and al-Qaeda: No Evidence of Alliance," *International Herald Tribune*, 19 February 2003.

22. Today, there is a small group of people who still believe that Saddam directed Osama bin Laden. Unsubstantiated comments based either on misinterpretation of information or on information derived during harsh interrogation remain uncorrected, propagating the myth. An Iraqi officer said, "Al-Qaeda's strong relationship with the Baath Party began in 1991 after Osama bin Laden visited with Saddam Hussein, the dictator, to collaborate between both parties." Interview, Iraqi Intelligence officer, February 2009.
23. Transcript of Powell's UN presentation, *CNN*, 6 February 2003.
24. Borzou Daragahi, "Islamic Militants Show Press the Camp Powell Called Poison Site," *Associated Press*, 8 February 2003.
25. Damien McElroy, "Chemical War Threat by Iraq's Taliban," *UK Telegraph*, 12 January 2003.
26. "Radical Islam in Iraqi Kurdistan: The Mouse That Roared?" ICG, Middle East Briefing No. 4, 7 February 2003.
27. *Ibid*.
28. Iraqi Support for Terrorism, CIA, September 2002: Ibn al-Shaykh is reported to have said that Iraq had "provided" chemical and biological weapons training for two al-Qaeda associates in 2000, but he "did not know the results of the training." Iraqi Support for Terrorism, CIA, January 2003: Ibn al-Shaykh is reported to have said, "Iraq — acting on the request of al-Qaida militant Abu Abdullah, who was Muhammad Atif's emissary — agreed to provide unspecified chemical or biological weapons training for two al-Qaida associates beginning in December 2000. The two individuals departed for Iraq but did not return, so al-Libi was not in a position to know if any training had taken place."
29. Transcript of Powell's UN presentation, *CNN*, 6 February 2003. The statement was repeated, both before and after the address to the world body. In Cincinnati in October 2002, Bush informed the public: "Iraq has trained al-Qaeda members in bomb making and poisons and gases."
30. Al-Libi indicated that his interrogators did not like his responses and then "placed him in a small box approximately 50 cm × 50 cm [20 inches × 20 inches]." He claimed he was held in the box for approximately 17 hours. When he was let out of the box, al-Libi claimed that

he was given a last opportunity to "tell the truth." When al-Libi did not satisfy the interrogator, al-Libi claimed that "he was knocked over with an arm thrust across his chest and he fell on his back." Al-Libi told CIA debriefers that he then "was punched for 15 minutes" (sourced to CIA cable, 5 February 2004).
31. *New York Times*, 5 November 2005, quoted two paragraphs of a Defense Intelligence Agency.
32. Jane Mayer, "Outsourcing Torture," *The New Yorker*, 14 February 2005.
33. Links between al-Qaeda and Kurdish Groups, Briefing by Security Service of Kurdistan, 14 February 2009.
34. *Ibid*. There are several photographs of these leaders in Afghanistan.
35. Interview, Head of Islamic Groups, Security Service of Kurdistan, 13 February 2009.
36. When Mohomed Sofi was killed three weeks after the formation of Kurdish Hamas, Abu Musab al Zarqawi, the leader of Tawhid Wal Jihad (later al-Qaeda in Iraq), appointed Omar Baziany as the Wali (Chief Amir) of Baghdad.
37. On 5 February 1999, after consultations with Congress, the US Administration designated in Presidential Determination 99–13 that the Islamic Movement of Kurdistan (IMK) was eligible to receive US military assistance under the ILA. The support is referenced in the State Department's report to Congress in June 2000 (CRS 98-179 F PDF file).
38. Sunil Ram, "The Enemy of My Enemy: The Odd Link between Ansar al Islam, Iraq and Iran," The Canadian Institute of Strategic Studies — Commentary, April 2002.
39. Jim Muir, "Al-Qaeda's Influence Grows in Iraq," *BBC News*, 24 July 2002.
40. Jonathan Schanzer, "Ansar al Islam: Back in Iraq," *Middle East Quarterly*, Vol. XI, No. 1 (Winter 2004).
41. Michael Ware, "Kurdistan: Death in the Afternoon," *Time*, 26 February 2003.
42. *Ibid*.
43. These estimates were based on debriefings of captured Ansar members. About 60 Ansar members were trained in Afghanistan.

44. Transcript of Powell's UN presentation, *CNN*, 6 February 2003. A Palestinian-Jordanian, Adnan Muhammad Sadik alias Abu Atia, was a graduate of Zarqawi's camp in Afghanistan and had served in Pankishi Valley in Georgia against the Russians in Chechnya. He was arrested in Azerbaijan and handed over to the CIA. Based on Abu Atia's interrogation, Powell remarked that at least nine North Africans were dispatched in 2001 to France, Britain, Spain, Italy, Germany, Russia, and elsewhere in Europe to conduct poison and explosive attacks. As of early 2003, 116 operatives had been arrested including the North African operatives. Andrew McGregor, "Ricin Fever: Abu Musab al Zarqawi in Pankisi Gorge," *Terrorism Monitor*, Jamestown Foundation, Vol. 2, No. 24 (15 December 2004).
45. An executive officer of the US Agency for International Development (USAID), Laurence Michael Foley, 62, was shot several times in the chest and head while walking towards his car in Amman, the capital of Jordan, on 28 October 2003. "US Diplomat Shot Dead in Jordan," *BBC*, 28 October 2002; and Jean-Charles Brisard and Damien Martinez, *Zarqawi, The New Face of Al-Qaeda* (New York: Other Press, 2005).
46. From Iraq, Abu Musab visited Syria in 2002, where he organized finance, weapons and training for his cell members in Syria, and arranged for their departure for Jordan with instructions. It is very likely that he also traveled to Jordan. Jamal Halaby, "11 Terror Suspects Charged in Jordan," *Associated Press*, via Boston Globe, 5 December 2002, http://www.boston.com/dailyglobe2/132/nation/11_terror_suspects_charged_in_Jordan+.shtml.
47. Rowan Scarborough, "US Tracked Top al-Qaeda Planner's Visit to Baghdad," *Washington Times*, 4 October 2002.
48. Interview, Sir John Scarlett, head, Secret Intelligence Service, UK, 2006. Before he became the head of SIS on 6 May 2004, Scarlett was chair of Joint Intelligence Committee. "JIC chief concedes he was aware of intelligence staff's worries over dossier," *The Independent*, UK, 24 September 2003.
49. Elizabeth Rubin, "The Battle for Beyara: A Year of Training for 12 Hours of Fighting in Northern Iraq," *Slate*, 3 April 2003.
50. Russell Skelton, "Need for that one final shot was fatal," *Herald*, 24 March 2003.

51. C.J. Chivers, "Terrorist manual may link Iraqi group to al-Qaeda: Information found at Ansar al Islam training center in Kurdish enclave," *New York Times*, 27 April 2003.
52. "Ansar al Islam Prepares for Suicide Attacks," *AFP, Daily Times*, Pakistan, 1 April 2003.
53. *Ibid.*
54. *Ibid.*
55. Eli J. Lake, "US Negotiates Trade of Terror Suspects," *The Washington Times*, 9 May 2003, http://washingtontimes.com/world/20030509-22822443.htm.
56. Elizabeth Rubin, "The Battle for Beyara: A Year of Training for 12 Hours of Fighting in Northern Iraq," *Slate*, 3 April 2003. "I asked him if the moderate Komala is any different from Ansar. 'After the American missile attacks, I assure you the number of fundamentalists in Komala increased from anger.'"
57. Elizabeth Rubin, "The Battle for Beyara: A Year of Training for 12 Hours of Fighting in Northern Iraq," *Slate*, 3 April 2003.
58. *Ibid.*
59. *Ibid.*
60. From Iran, Krekar moved to Norway, where he and his family were granted refugee status in 1993 through the United Nations refugee resettlement program. While in Norway, he founded and served as an Imam for the Islamic Vision of Norway. Mullah Krekar was briefly detained in the Netherlands in September 2002, but managed to relocate to Norway where he continued to manage a robust Ansar network in Scandinavia.
61. http://www.defenselink.mil/news/newsarticle.aspx?id=15837.
62. Jean-Charles Brisard and Damien Martinez, *The New Face of Al-Qaeda* (New York: Other Press, 2005). This book provides the most detailed account of the group.
63. In addition to coalition forces and foreign diplomats, al-Qaeda in Iraq targeted national and provincial government officials, especially military and police personnel, professionals, and academics.
64. "Statement of Mujahidin Shura Council on Establishment of 'Islamic State of Iraq,'" Jihadist Websites — OSC Report, 15 October 2006.

65. "Al-Qaeda in Iraq Hampered by Bureaucracy and Loss of Sunni Support," United States Military Academy at West Point, 20 April 2006.
66. According to classical Islamic sources, Hilf al-Mutayyabin was an oath of allegiance taken in pre-Islamic times by several clans of the Quraysh tribe, in which they undertook to protect the oppressed and the wronged. The name "Oath of the Scented Ones" apparently derived from the fact that the participants sealed the oath by dipping their hands in perfume and then rubbing them over the Ka'ba. This practice was later adopted by the Prophet Muhammad and incorporated into Islam.
67. ICPVTR Middle East Annual Assessment 2006.
68. "Jihadist Website Posts Full English Transcript of Latest Al-Zawahiri Video," Jihadist Websites — OSC Report, 21 December 2006.
69. "Zarqawi Died of Blast Injuries," *BBC*, 12 June 2006; and http://www.centcom.mil/sites/uscentcom2/Exposing%20the%20Enemy/Al-Zarqawi's%20Successor.aspx.
70. Unlike Abu Musab, Abu Ayyub maintained a low profile. Interview with high-value detainees, Camp Cropper, December 2006, http://usinfo.state.gov/mena/Archive/2006/Jun/16-439007.html.
71. "Identity of Zarqawi's Successor Still a Riddle," *AFP*, 18 June 2006.
72. "Al-Muhajir Pledges Allegiance to Al-Baghdadi, Threatens US, Europe," Jihadist Websites — OSC Report, 11 November 2006.
73. Abu Ayyub followed Abu Musab's tradition of extensive use of multi-media communication. His messages aimed to galvanize the Iraqis and terrorize the US. In an audio speech posted on the Internet on 28 September 2006, he even called for the use of dirty bombs against US bases in Iraq. Furthermore, in an Internet message on 10 November 2006, Abu Ayyub threatened the US and Europe.
74. "Amir Gives Speech, Asks Each Muslim to Kill One American in 15 Days," Jihadist Websites — OSC Report, 8 September 2006; and "Mujahidin Shura Council Issues Abu Hamzah al-Muhajir Audio Calling for Use of Dirty Bombs against US Bases in Iraq," Jihadist Websites — OSC Report, 29 September 2006.
75. Interview with a member of al-Qaeda in Iraq, *BBC*, 18 September 2006.

76. "Iraq Chiefs Vow to Fight al-Qaeda," Iraq — OSC Report, 28 September 2006; "Al-Anbar Salvation Council Al-Anbar Awakening Council Iraqi Televisions Highlight Al-Anbar Chieftains' Meeting With Al-Maliki" and "Iraq Tribal Leaders Vow to Fight Terrorist Groups," Radio Free Europe, 27 September 2006.
77. http://www.wna-news.com/inanews/news.php?item.2365.15.
78. "Iraq Tribe Says It Kills Dozens of Qaeda Fighters," *Reuters*, 26 November 2006.
79. *Ibid.*
80. "Al-Qaeda's outrages swing Sunnis to US," *UPI*, 17 February 2007.
81. *Ibid.*
82. "Attacks Kill 30 in Iraq, Mourners Gunned Down," *Reuters*, 19 February 2007.
83. "Blast May Hint at Growing Sunni Conflict," *AP*, 25 February 2007.
84. http://www1.nefafoundation.org/miscellaneous/iaidigest1107-1.pdf.
85. http://nefafoundation.org/miscellaneous/FeaturedDocs/nefabaghdadi0907.pdf.
86. http://www1.nefafoundation.org/miscellaneous/FeaturedDocs/nefahamasiraq0308.pdf.
87. http://www1.nefafoundation.org/miscellaneous/FeaturedDocs/nefahamasiraq0308.pdf.
88. http://canadiancoalition.com/forum/messages/19503.shtml.
89. http://www.nefafoundation.org/miscellaneous/mustafaarmy0408.pdf.
90. "Kurdistan Brigades Pledges Allegiance to Al Qaeda-led Group, Internet, Terror Monitor," *CBS News*, 6 October 2008.
91. "The Shura Council of the Bubaz Tribes Issues a Statement of Reconciliation to the Mujahideen Groups in Iraq, namely, the Mujahideen Shura Council," Site Institute, 6 October 2006.
92. Mark Perry, "US Military Breaks Ranks: A Salvo at the White House," http://www.atimes.com/atimes/Middle_East/JA24Ak02.html.
93. *Ibid.*
94. Brendan Minite, "The Fallujah Brigade: How the Marines are Pacifying an Iraqi Hot Spot," *The Wall Street Journal*, 1 June 2004. To quote Col. Coleman: "What they needed to do was drive wedges into the enemy ranks — divide and conquer. From studying the enemy, the

Marines realized the insurgents can be separated into five disparate groups with widely varying goals: foreign fighters (some of whom are very skilled bomb makers), religious extremists, violent criminals released from prison by Saddam and willing to kill for money, Saddam loyalists [those Col. Coleman described as "bloody up to their elbows" in the old regime], and former military personnel."

95. Mark Perry, "US Military Breaks Ranks: A Salvo at the White House," http://www.atimes.com/atimes/Middle_East/JA24Ak02.html.
96. Ibid.
97. Ibid.
98. Ibid.
99. Alissa J. Rubin and Damien Cave, "In a Force for Iraqi Calm, Seeds of Conflict," *New York Times*, 23 December 2007.
100. "Awakening Movement in Iraq," *New York Times*, 20 April 2009; and Mike Lanchin and Mona Mahmoud, "Iraq Signs Up to Awakening Movement," *BBC*, Baghdad, 4 February 2008.
101. For instance, under Major General Douglas Stone (the head of Iraq's rehabilitation program), the US rehabilitated and released over 10,000 detainees, which informed Iraqis that the US meant well. Interview, Douglas Stone, 24 February 2009.
102. inSITE: State of the Insurgency in Iraq, January 2009, 21 February 2009.
103. Ibid.
104. Ibid.
105. *Ibid*. Through al-Fajr Media Center on 9 January, ISI leader Abu Omar al-Baghdadi urged Palestinians, particularly those outside Gaza, to strike US, Israeli and Arab interests. On 15 January, Ansar al Islam stressed that only jihad through guerilla warfare and launching of rockets will affect change in Palestine, not democracy and diplomacy.
106. http://sitemultimedia.org/docs/inSITE_Afghanistan_Jan2009.pdf, 11 March 2009.
107. Ibid.

# Index

9/11  38, 39, 42, 55–57, 68–71, 80, 89, 119, 138

Afghanistan  3, 11, 40, 47, 56, 80, 95, 96, 109–111, 113, 114, 116–122, 124, 127, 135, 137–139
al-Qaeda  12, 110, 111, 115, 137, 138
al-Qaeda in Iraq  7, 10, 11, 111, 112, 125–134
Ansar al Islam  10, 11, 112, 119, 120, 122–125
Arabs  21–23, 26, 28, 49, 57, 113, 114, 118, 121, 124, 131

bin Laden, Osama  13, 110, 113–116, 118, 121, 122, 126
Bush administration  3, 4, 8, 28, 32, 50, 69, 70, 115, 137
   invasion in 2003  1–4, 18, 66–71, 109, 110, 115–117, 137
   post-invasion policy  28, 29, 32, 132–136

unilateralism  89, 90, 107
war on terror  3, 38–40, 66, 93

China  2, 9, 60, 67, 87, 93, 104–106, 119
cosmopolitanism  10, 98–100

democratization/political reform  8, 42, 50, 51, 58, 59

ethno-sectarian identity politics  7, 19–24
European Union (EU)  9, 55, 61, 87, 89, 92, 100, 105

global governance  5, 6, 10, 12, 85, 89–96, 98, 99, 101, 106, 107
   crisis in  6, 10, 92–98
   nature of  90–92

Hamas  39, 40, 43–45, 47, 57, 118, 119, 129, 136
human rights  4, 25, 71, 79, 85, 86, 90, 95, 99, 100, 104

# 150  Index

Hussein, Saddam  1, 3, 5, 7, 12, 13, 17, 18, 20–22, 26, 32, 47, 65, 67–70, 95, 111, 114, 117, 119, 122, 137

International Monetary Fund (IMF)  32, 87–89, 91, 94
Iran  5, 10, 17, 22, 24, 29, 30, 35, 36, 38–40, 43, 44, 46, 52–55, 57, 59, 61, 63, 70, 89, 94, 95, 111, 114, 117, 119–123, 127, 132, 135
Islamic Movement in Kurdistan (IMK)  11, 111–114, 117–119
Islamic State of Iraq (ISI)  11, 27, 111, 112, 126–134
Israel  3–5, 12, 36, 39–41, 43–48, 51, 55–59, 61, 63, 66, 67, 70, 71, 94, 104, 136

Jordan  25, 39, 42, 47, 50, 56, 59, 113, 121, 122, 133

Kurds  19–24, 26

Lebanon  36, 39, 41, 43–45, 53, 54, 57, 94, 122, 127
liberalism  8, 31–33, 72–74, 76–78, 81–84
  economic ideology  31, 32
  political ideology  72–79
  problems  6, 9, 10, 81–84
  *zeitgeist*  9, 72–78

multilateralism  10, 89, 101, 102

neo-conservatives  4
neo-liberalism, *see* liberalism  31–33

non-governmental organizations (NGOs)  13, 91, 92, 96, 99, 106
North Atlantic Treaty Organization (NATO)  2, 3, 21, 55, 85, 87, 89, 93, 96

Obama administration  29, 30, 62
oil issues  3, 4, 70, 137

Palestine Liberation Organization (PLO)  38, 50
political reform, *see* democratization  8, 42, 50–52
programmatic politics  7, 12, 19–24

Rumsfeld, Donald  4, 69, 83
Russia  2, 9, 60, 67, 89, 93, 104

Saudi Arabia  8, 38, 39, 42, 45, 47, 50, 55, 56, 58, 59, 70, 71, 122, 138
Shia  19–24
Sunni  19–24, 27, 28, 133, 134
Syria  22, 25, 26, 35, 39, 40, 43–45, 50, 52, 54, 55, 57, 63, 122, 133

Tawhid Wal Jihad  11, 112, 124, 125
Turkey  17, 22, 30, 45, 51, 55, 58, 59

United Kingdom  68
United Nations (UN)  61, 62, 67, 68, 86–88, 94–96
  *An Agenda for Peace*  86, 94

General Assembly   2, 98, 103–105
peacekeeping operations   103
reform   10, 12, 13, 103–106
Security Council   2, 10, 68, 86, 87, 89, 94, 102–104, 115

weapons of mass destruction (WMDs)   3, 5, 12, 46, 68, 69, 71, 93, 115, 116, 138
World Trade Organization (WTO)   32, 33, 87–89, 91

www.ingramcontent.com/pod-product-compliance
Lightning Source LLC
Chambersburg PA
CBHW051118230426
43667CB00014B/2639